ParKit Golf

Encyclopedia of Fun Golf Games

By Rick Heard, PGA
Don Law, PGA
Bill Scott, PGA

Visit our website at www.parkitgolf.com

Published by ARD Publishing
Boca Raton, Florida

Printed in the United States of America

ISBN-13: 978-0-9913557-0-9

ParKit Golf

Encyclopedia of Fun Golf Games

PARKIT GOLF ENCYCLOPEDIA OF FUN GOLF GAMES

CONTENTS

CONTENTS

PARKIT GOLF ENCYCLOPEDIA OF FUN GOLF GAMES

CONTENTS

CONTENTS

PARKIT GOLF ENCYCLOPEDIA OF FUN GOLF GAMES

CONTENTS

CONTENTS

CONTENTS

PARKIT GOLF ENCYCLOPEDIA OF FUN GOLF GAMES

CONTENTS

INTRODUCTION

If you want to improve your golf game, there are no shortcuts. You must practice, and you must practice the right areas. It sounds difficult, and it is, but practice does not have to be boring! Through our extensive work teaching both juniors and adults, we have developed many fun, skill-based games that convert boring practice drills into fun activities.

The ParKit Golf Encyclopedia of Fun Golf Games is a compilation of 50 individual and team golf games for golfers of all ages and abilities. The *Encyclopedia* can be used by golf professionals and coaches who teach groups of kids or adults, by parents coaching their kids, and by individual golfers seeking to improve their skills.

The games include both individual and team competitions that convert ordinary, boring practice exercises into fun activities. Through the fun and excitement of playing these fantastic games, players will learn the techniques and fundamentals of all of the major elements of golf. Far beyond simply competing with others and themselves, players will learn to control their golf ball in putting, chipping, pitching, bunkers, and full swing shots. And, in playing the games, they will learn golf etiquette, sportsmanship and respect for others.

Each game is explained in clear language that is simple to follow and understand. The games are appropriate for junior golf camps, group programs, adult classes, and for individual students at all levels. Many of the games may be played in an open field or other non golf course location, and even indoors if a golf course practice facility is not available.

In this book you will find complete instructions for playing all 50 practice games. Many of the games use tools and supporting materials that help focus on a target or help organize participants for safety. These tools and materials can be found at ParKit Golf's website www.parkitgolf.com.

As you learn these games, you will find that most of them may be played in many different variations. Although some may seem designed for one discipline, most of the games apply to several different situations. The table of contents shows a cross-reference for each game, showing how they may apply to putting, chipping, pitching, bunkers, approach shots, and full shots. In addition, some games focus on distance control, which is paramount for most junior golfers. Lastly, many games may be played indoors, while some are appropriate for on the golf course. Most games may be played with multiple players or individually.

We encourage you to adapt the games to fit your needs, and develop your own variations of them to customize them for your teaching or learning requirements.

The ParKit Golf Encyclopedia of Fun Golf Games reflects the experience and wisdom of the ParKit Golf team. Owned and operated by PGA golf professionals and staff with a passion for junior golf, ParKit Golf is the authoritative source for products, services and information related to junior golf instruction. With more than 90 years of combined experience in creating and teaching innovative junior golf programs to thousands of junior golfers, ParKit Golf represents one of the most experienced junior golf leadership teams in the world.

Equipment and Supplies Needed

Most of the games described in *The ParKit Golf Encyclopedia of Fun Golf Games* make use of props and tools to make the games more enjoyable or, in the case of multiple player games, for safety. Some games require special equipment. Below is a compilation of all of the equipment and supplies needed for all of the games in this book. All of these items are available directly from ParKit Golf, Inc. through the ParKit Golf website at www.parkitgolf.com.

- Game scoring pad
- Colored cones (8)
- ParZone aiming rings (18", 3', 6', and 12' rings). Tic Tac Golf requires nine of the 3' rings for easiest setup and play.
- Ball markers (2)
- Colored golf balls (16; 4 each of orange, blue, green, and yellow, plus other colors as desired)
- Cow ball (1), 8-ball (1) and striped ball (1)
- Assorted novelty balls for prizes or for fun playing games
- Long roll of colored string
- ParKit wickets (4 sizes: 1-point wickets (5), 3-point wicket (1), 5-point wicket (1), and 7-point wicket (1)
- Aiming sticks and connectors
- Colorful pool foam noodle
- ParKit Golf Bingo pad
- Alphabet letter cards
- Easel
- Portable whiteboard & dry erase markers
- Putting pins (2)
- Pink Plank
- Putt n' Spin spinner
- Rules flashcards
- Game tokens (4)
- 6" inflatable beach balls (12)
- Mini soccer balls
- Plastic range baskets (6)

ParKit Golf

Encyclopedia of Fun Golf Games

"21 OR BUST"

Overview: This game for 1 or more players helps develop:

- ✓ Directional control
- ✓ Strategy
- ✓ Mathematical thinking

Equipment Required:

- ✓ 4 ParKit Golf "21" Wickets
- ✓ 2 ParKit Golf ball markers
- ✓ ParKit Golf scoring pad
- ✓ 1 ParKit Golf cone

Setup: Please refer to the drawing on the facing page.

➢ Insert each ParKit "21" wicket into the putting green (push wicket in approximately 2 inches). Arrange the "21" wickets in a line, leaving about 6 inches between wickets. You may place the wickets in any order by size.

➢ Place the ParKit ball markers about 3 feet apart and approximately 6-8 feet from the "21" wickets.

➢ Place the ParKit cone where players will await their turn.

How To Play:

- Determine the order of play among the players. This order will be kept throughout the game. Players wait behind the "on-deck" cone until it is their turn. While waiting, players must hold their putter by the head, and display good golf etiquette.

- Each player putts from between the ball markers toward the "21"wickets. The "21" wickets are valued at 1 point, 3 points, 5 points, and 7 points. The player decides which wicket to aim for and attempts to putt through the wicket.

"21 OR BUST"

- If the ball goes through a wicket, the player will receive the point value for that wicket. If any part of the ball goes through a wicket, the player will receive that point value.

- The winner is the first player to reach exactly 21 points.

- If a player goes over 21 points, he "busts" and his point total is reset to 11.

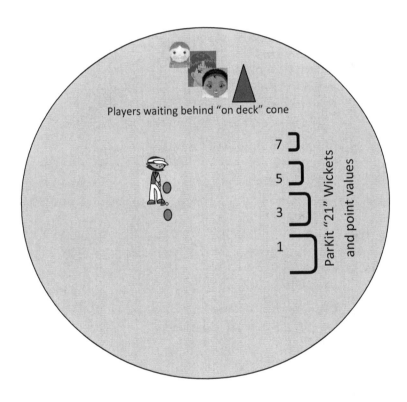

321-SCORE!

Overview: "321-Score!" is a way of keeping score in practice rounds that will help you focus on starting and finishing strong. It also helps to simulate the pressure situations that arise during competitive golf.

Equipment Required:

✓ No special equipment is required other than a regular scorecard.

Setup: Please refer to the example on the facing page.

➢ Using a regular scorecard, write the "321" multiplier numbers on the card as shown.

➢ Calculate the "321 Par" for your course by multiplying the "321" multiplier by the course par for each hole.

How To Play:

Play a nine-hole round of golf, following USGA rules as though you were playing in a tournament. In addition to keeping your regular score, also keep your "321" score by using the "321" multiplier.

If your score for the first hole is a 5, your "321" score is 15 (5 times the "321" multiplier of 3). So, using the "321" multiplier, you will count the first hole three times. Count the second hole twice. Count holes three through five only once each. Count holes six and seven twice each. Finally, count holes eight and nine three times each.

This way, your nine holes will be counted as 18 holes, and your 18 hole score will depend on how well you start and finish.

Your "par" for 18 holes using the "321" multiplier will not necessarily be the same as the regular par for your 18 hole course. This happens due to the location of par 3, par 4, and par 5 holes on your course. It is not a problem if your "321" par ends up being different than your regular par.

321-SCORE!

Hole	1	2	3	4	5	6	7	8	9	TOT
Yards	475	160	390	410	375	170	525	393	382	3280
Par	5	3	4	4	4	3	5	4	4	36
321 Multiplier	3	2	1	1	1	2	2	3	3	
321 "Par"	15	6	4	4	4	6	10	12	12	73
Actual Score	5	4	4	5	3	3	4	4	5	37
321 Score	15	8	4	5	3	6	8	12	15	76

Sample "321" Scorecard Instructions

Write the "321" multiplier values on your scorecard for each hole, as shown above.

Calculate the "321" par for your course by multiplying the "321" multiplier by the course par for each hole.

Keep your own actual score for each hole as usual.

Calculate your "321" score by multiplying the "321" multiplier by your actual score.

ACE OF CLUBS

Overview: This game may be played by any number of players or teams in a wide variety of situations on or around the green. Ace of Clubs helps to develop:

✓ Shotmaking direction and distance control

Equipment Required:

✓ 6 ParKit Golf cones
✓ ParKit Golf scoring pad
✓ 3 ParZone target rings

Setup: Please refer to the drawing on the facing page.

➤ Create two starting stations by placing 2 ParKit cones 6 feet apart for each station. Choose the starting location appropriate for the type of shot to be used (e.g. putt, chip, pitch) and the skill level of the players. Place a ParKit cone where players will await their turn at each station.

➤ Place three different size ParZone rings: small ring for a short chip; medium ring for a medium chip, and large ring for a long chip.

How To Play:

➤ Play individually or create teams (need not be equal sized). Provide an equal number of golf balls (e.g., 10 balls) to each team or side. Determine which team or side is to play first.

➤ Each team will determine their own order of play. Players wait behind the "on-deck" cone until it is their turn.

➤ Alternating shots between teams or sides, each player will chip one ball toward the ParZone ring of their choice, scoring points if the ball comes to rest inside a ring. Score as follows: 1 point

ACE OF CLUBS

for the small ring; 2 points for the medium ring; and 3 points for the large ring.

➤ When all balls have been chipped, the round ends. The winner is the team or side with the most points. Ties may be broken by continuing to alternate between teams or sides until one team or side scores more points.

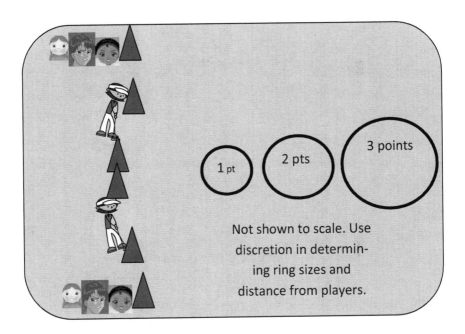

1 pt

2 pts

3 points

Not shown to scale. Use discretion in determining ring sizes and distance from players.

AIR MAIL

Overview: Air Mail is a more challenging version of "Catch Me (If You Can)." Air Mail helps develop chipping and pitching and bunker technique and distance control, and can also be used for full shots. The object is to make each ball fly farther in the air than the prior ball without going past a maximum distance boundary.

Equipment Required:

- ✓ Supply of golf balls (either regular balls or range balls)
- ✓ 2 ball markers or tees

Setup: Please refer to the drawing on the facing page.

➤ Create a starting point by placing 2 ball markers or tees 6 feet apart in an area suitable for chipping, pitching or bunker shots.

➤ Create an out-of-bounds limit so that the game will end when a ball travels beyond the limit. This could be the edge of the green, a string stretched across the green, or some other area. This limit should be about 35 yards away from the starting point.

How To Play:

➤ The goal is to hit (either a chip, pitch, or bunker shot) as many balls in a row as possible where each ball flies farther in the air than the prior ball ("target ball") without going beyond the "out-of-bounds" limit. Each ball must "air mail" the target ball.

➤ Each player begins by hitting a ball a short distance, scoring 1 point. That ball becomes the target ball for the next shot. The player then hits a second ball. If that ball flies over the target ball and stops before going out-of-bounds, score another point and that ball becomes the new target ball.

➤ If the ball lands on top of the target ball, the shot scores a point and the new target ball is whichever ball comes to rest farther from the player.

AIR MAIL

➤ Continue hitting until a ball either fails to air mail the target ball or the ball goes too far (out-of-bounds). Score a point each time the ball air mails the target ball and stays in bounds.

➤ If playing individually, keep a record of the number of points you score, and attempt to set a new record each time you play the game.

➤ If competing with multiple players, the winner is the player with the most points, once all players have had an equal number of turns.

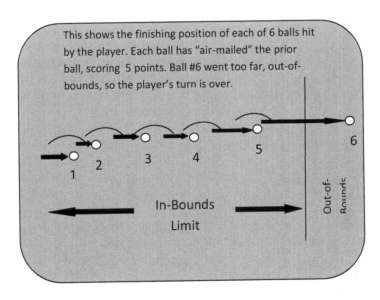

This shows the finishing position of each of 6 balls hit by the player. Each ball has "air-mailed" the prior ball, scoring 5 points. Ball #6 went too far, out-of-bounds, so the player's turn is over.

In-Bounds Limit

Out-of-Bounds

1   2   3   4   5   6

BATTER UP!

Overview: Batter Up! can be used for all short game situations, and is excellent for practicing both distance and directional control. The object is to be able to repeat your swing and be able to hit each ball to the same spot on the green. You can hit it there once... can you do it again and again?

Equipment Required:

- ✓ 3' and 6' ParZone rings
- ✓ 10 golf balls, including 1 colored ball

Setup: Please refer to the drawing on the facing page.

➤ Select a flat area of the putting green away from any hole.

➤ Place the 10 balls together either on the green (if putting) or off the green (if chipping, pitching, or hitting bunker shots).

➤ Set the ParZone rings aside until all 10 balls have been hit.

How To Play:

➤ The object of the game is to achieve the highest possible "batting average" by consistently hitting the 10 balls to the same spot.

➤ Begin by hitting the colored ball toward an open area on the green (not toward a hole).

➤ Pay close attention to where this colored ball comes to rest. Then, continue hitting the nine remaining balls, trying to make each ball come to rest in the exact same place as the colored ball.

➤ After you have hit all 10 balls, select either the 3' or 6' ParZone ring and place it over the largest cluster of balls that includes the colored ball.

➤ Count the number of balls that are within the ring and multiply this number by 100; that is your "batting average."

BATTER UP!

➤ Keep a record of your batting average, and attempt to set a new record each time you play the game.

➤ If competing with multiple players, the winner is the player with the highest batting average.

➤ If the ParZone ring is too small to frequently encircle more than one ball, use the larger ring until your skill level improves.

➤ Try this game blindfolded! After hitting the first ball, close your eyes or wear a blindfold and see how well you do.

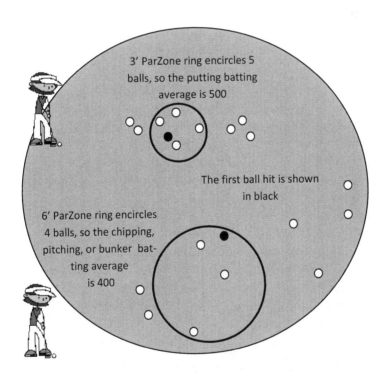

3' ParZone ring encircles 5 balls, so the putting batting average is 500

The first ball hit is shown in black

6' ParZone ring encircles 4 balls, so the chipping, pitching, or bunker batting average is 400

BULLSEYE

Overview: Bullseye is for 1 or more players and helps develop:

- ✓ Chipping technique
- ✓ Direction and distance control

Equipment Required:

- ✓ 2-4 ParZone rings
- ✓ ParKit Golf scoring pad
- ✓ 3 ParKit Golf cones

Setup: Please refer to the drawing on the facing page.

- ➢ Place the different sized ParZone rings around a hole on the putting or chipping green, starting with the smallest ring.

- ➢ Assign point values to the circles: in the hole is 25 points, smallest circle is 15 points, next circle is 10 points, next circle is 5 points, and largest circle is 1 point (the point assignments and number of circles used may be changed as needed).

- ➢ Place 2 ParKit cones about 6 feet apart, off the green in the area to be used for chipping.

- ➢ Place the other ParKit cone where players will await their turn.

How To Play:

- Determine the order of play among the players. This order will be kept throughout the game. Players wait behind the "on-deck" cone until it is their turn.

- Each player chips 5 balls from between the starting cones toward the hole surrounded by rings. Keep a running total of the points scored by the player.

- After the player chips 5 balls, the next player takes his turn.

BULLSEYE

- The winner is the first player to reach 100 points (or another point total determined by the instructor), once all players have had an equal number of turns (i.e., when a player reaches 100 points, any remaining players after him in the round each get a final chance).

- Variation: Use five different chipping stations around the green and assign each player to a station. Each player chips 5 balls, tallies their points, then rotates to the next station. This continues until each player has chipped from each station. The winner is the player with the highest point total after completing the rotation.

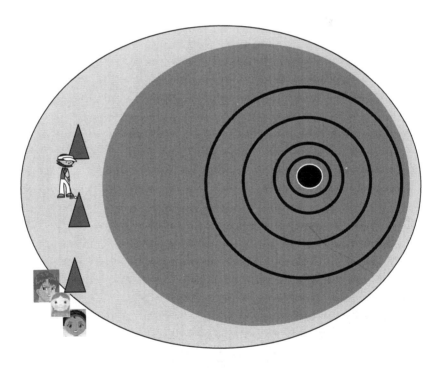

CADDY SWAP

Overview: Caddy Swap can be an eye-opener that changes your outlook on how you play golf. The concept is simple: play a round of golf with your regular golf partner or any other person. Just for this round, agree ahead of time to "caddy" for one another.

The goal is to see the course, and your playing strategy, from a different perspective. Seeing the course through someone else's eyes, and playing shots according to their way of thinking can enhance the way you play and help improve your course management skills.

Caddy Swap is for 2 players and helps develop:

✓ Club selection strategy
✓ Shot making strategy

Equipment Required:

✓ No special equipment is required… just a cooperative golf buddy who is willing to assist you and be assisted by you.

Setup: No special setup is required. Just play golf with your golf buddy as your caddy.

How To Play:

Go to the course with an open mind and a golf buddy who is willing to try a different approach for nine holes. Agree ahead of time on your roles for the nine holes. In each person's role as caddy, he or she will do the best interpretation of a professional tour caddy (except for carrying the bag!). The caddy provides advice on shot strategy, club selection, and always keeps a positive attitude and instills confidence in his or her player. Your goal as caddy in Caddy Swap is to guide the player and suggest that they play the course as you would play it.

CADDY SWAP

The player is ultimately responsible for each shot, but seeks and listens to advice and counsel from his or her caddy. For this round using Caddy Swap, your goal as player is to always follow the shot strategy suggested by the caddy, using the club mutually agreed upon by caddy and player.

When the round is over, think back to your round and the types of shots you played, and consider these questions:

- Were the shots you played different than how you would usually approach them?

- Did you use the same clubs you would usually use, or did you use a stronger club? How did that work out for you?

- Are you usually more conservative or more aggressive in how you play the course than you were when following the advice of your caddy?

- Did you find yourself trying the opposite approach sometimes, and if so, did that help or hurt your score?

- Lastly, did it help to have a "teammate" who kept a positive attitude and tried to keep you positive?

CATCH ME (IF YOU CAN)

Overview: Catch Me (If You Can) helps develop distance control for all types of shots, including putting, chipping, pitching, bunkers, and even full shots. The object is simple: hit each ball farther than the prior ball – as many times as possible.

Equipment Required:

- ✓ Supply of golf balls (either regular balls or range balls)
- ✓ 2 ball markers or tees

Setup: Please refer to the drawing on the facing page.

➢ Create a starting point by placing 2 ball markers or tees 6 feet apart either on the green (for putting) or in an area suitable for chipping, pitching, bunkers or full shots.

➢ Create an out-of-bounds limit so that the game will end when a ball travels beyond the limit. For putting, this could be the edge of the green, a string stretched across the green, or some other area. For chipping, pitching, and bunkers, this could be a line about 25 yards away from the starting point. For full shots it could be a yardage marker.

How To Play:

➢ The goal is to hit as many balls in a row as possible where each ball travels farther than the prior ball ("target ball") without going beyond the "out-of-bounds" limit. Each ball must "catch up to" the target ball.

➢ Each player begins by hitting a ball a short distance, scoring 1 point. That ball becomes the target ball for the next shot. The player then hits a second ball. If that ball catches or passes the target ball, score another point and that ball becomes the new target ball for the next shot.

CATCH ME (IF YOU CAN)

> ➢ If the ball strikes the target ball, the shot scores a point and the new target ball is whichever ball comes to rest farther from the player.

> ➢ Continue hitting until a ball either fails to catch the target ball or the ball goes too far (out-of-bounds). Score a point each time the ball catches or passes the target ball.

> ➢ If playing individually, keep a record of the number of points you score, and attempt to set a new record each time you play the game.

> ➢ If competing with multiple players, the winner is the player with the most points, once all players have had an equal number of turns.

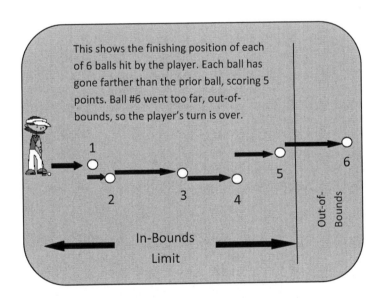

33

CLOCKWORK

Overview: Clockwork is a circle putting drill that focuses on short putts (usually 2nd putts) from all angles around the hole. The object is to sink as many putts in a row as possible, working your way around the hole like the hands of a clock.

Equipment Required:

- ✓ Up to 12 golf balls
- ✓ 3' and 6' ParZone target rings

Setup: Please refer to the drawing on the facing page.

➤ For short putts, place the 6' ParZone ring around a hole on the putting green and place 6 golf balls in a circle around the hole, using the ring as a guide in placing the balls. Space the balls evenly as shown in the diagram. Remove the ring when all balls are in place.

➤ For long putts, use the 3' ParZone ring as a target instead of the hole, and place up to 12 golf balls in a circle the desired distance from the ParZone target ring (e.g. 20').

How To Play:

➤ Beginning with any ball, putt toward the hole (or ParZone ring, depending on the above setup).

➤ If the ball is holed or (for long putts) finishes in the ParZone target ring, continue putting the next ball. If the ball is not holed or does not finish within the ParZone target ring, the player's turn ends and the balls are reset for the next player or next round. Continue putting, adding more balls as necessary, until a putt misses the hole (or ParZone ring).

CLOCKWORK

> Score one point for each ball that is either holed or finishes inside the ParZone target rings.

> If playing individually, keep a record of the number of points you score, and attempt to set a new record each time you play the game.

> If competing with multiple players, the winner is the player with the most points, once all players have had an equal number of turns.

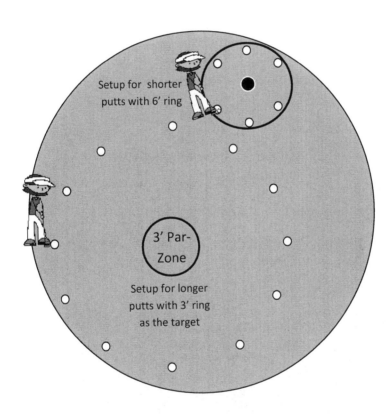

CLUBSTER

Overview: Clubster is a chipping game for one or more players. As with many things in life, there are two paths to choose from: the easy way and the hard way. Most of us prefer to do things the easy way, but when it comes to chipping, many people unknowingly choose the hard way and use the sand wedge for every shot. That can work, but the sand wedge is often the most difficult club to use for chipping, since we usually want the ball to stay low and roll most of the way to the hole.

Think of your set of clubs as 14 tools that you can use to get a job done. The job is to get your ball in or close to the hole. Your challenge is to select the right tool (club) for the job, depending on where your ball lies, the distance to the hole, the slope of the green, the speed of the green, and other factors. If you use the right club, the job is easier. If you use the wrong club, it can be much more difficult. So, how do you find out which club is the best one for you to use for each type of shot? Clubster can help you figure it out. And remember, the right club for you might not be the right club for someone else.

Equipment Required:

✓ Each player should bring his or her sand wedge, gap wedge, pitching wedge, 9-iron, 8-iron, and 7-iron. Also, each player will each need five marked golf balls.

Setup: Please refer to the drawing on the facing page. Also refer to the Clubster scorecard on the following page.

How To Play:

Multiple Player Rules: No two players can use the same club at the same time. In other words, someone uses the sand wedge, someone else uses the pitching wedge, someone else uses the 9-iron, and so on. Select a starting location for a chip shot from around the green. Select a target hole to chip to. Each player gets three tries, and only the best of the three shots counts. The person who gets the ball closest to the hole wins, but record which club they used (see sample scorecard below).

CLUBSTER

After each series, rotate clubs so that everyone changes to the next higher club and tries again. Record the distance in feet (estimate or measure) for the club that is the best in each series and see if there is a pattern. Do the high-lofted clubs or the low-lofted clubs "win" more often?

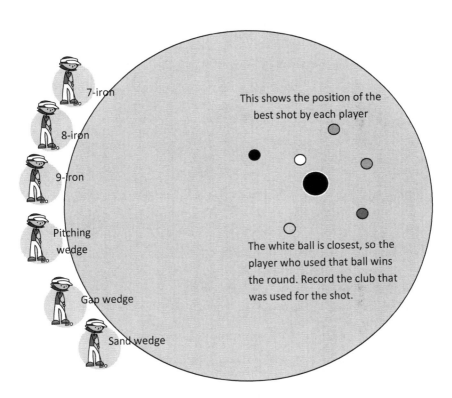

7-iron

8-iron

9-iron

Pitching wedge

Gap wedge

Sand wedge

This shows the position of the best shot by each player

The white ball is closest, so the player who used that ball wins the round. Record the club that was used for the shot.

CLUBSTER

Variations: Single Player Rules: This form of Clubster is a personal challenge to see how good you can be with each club. After all, an accomplished golfer should have the skills to get the ball close to the hole using many different clubs. Take the same six clubs listed above and select a starting location and target as above. Make a scorecard by listing the name of each club as shown below.

Then, hit five balls with each club, trying to hit your best shot each time. When you have finished all five balls for a particular club, walk up to the target hole and add up the total distance from the hole to the best three shots. For example, if the best three shots are 1 foot, 3 feet, and 4 feet away from the hole, your total is 8 feet. You can either estimate the distances or use a tape measure. Write that total down next to the club on your scorecard.

When you have done this for each club, compare the total distances and see which club was best for you for this particular shot. Try this from several different locations and see if you see patterns in which club is best. You may find that one club is best for several different types of shots. You may also find that high-lofted clubs are better for some shots, while low-lofted clubs are better for others.

CLUBSTER

					9	8	7
Try #	Player	Sand Wedge	Gap Wedge	Pitching Wedge	Iron	Iron	Iron
1							
2							
3							
4							
5							
6							

CLUBSTER CHIPPING GAME SCORECARD

CLUB TRICKS

Overview: Club Tricks helps you learn that you can successfully hit a shot with many different clubs. The object is to learn to use a variety of clubs for a particular shot, and ultimately to be able to select the best club for each situation. For any given shot, you may have a choice of several clubs. You should always try to choose the easiest and most reliable club for each shot.

Equipment Required:

- ✓ 6' ParZone ring
- ✓ 12 colored golf balls – 4 each in 3 colors
- ✓ Selection of golf clubs (e.g., sand wedge, wedge, and 8-iron)

Setup: Please refer to the drawing on the facing page.

➤ Select an area of the putting green away from any hole and place the 6' ParZone ring on the green.

➤ Place the 12 balls off the green in 3 color-coded groups, each with 4 balls.

How To Play:

➤ The object of the game is to hit all 12 balls into the ParZone target ring, using three different clubs for the same shot. In doing so, you will learn how to control your ball with different clubs. You will also learn which clubs are best for certain types of shots.

➤ Begin by selecting a club and hitting the first four colored balls toward the ParZone target ring. Pay attention to how easy or difficult it is to hit the balls into the ParZone ring. Your goal is to learn which club is the easiest to use for the situation.

➤ After hitting the first four balls, select a different club and repeat the above with the next four colored balls. Using the third club, repeat again with the remaining colored balls.

CLUB TRICKS

➢ Compare the number of balls that were within the target ring for each club. Pay attention to which group of balls are the least consistent or farthest from the target ring.

➢ Replace the club that produced the worst results with a different club and repeat the entire game from the same situation.

➢ Through the process of elimination, discover the club that is the easiest to use for the situation.

➢ Keep a record of which clubs are the easiest to use in different situation

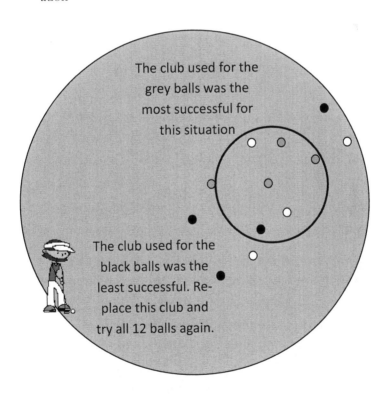

The club used for the grey balls was the most successful for this situation

The club used for the black balls was the least successful. Replace this club and try all 12 balls again.

COW PASTURE POOL

Overview: This game may be played by 2 or more players. Putting's version of billiards, Cow Pasture Pool helps the student develop:

- ✓ Overall putting skills
- ✓ Strategy and risk-reward thinking in planning the next shot

Equipment Required:

- ✓ 4 ParKit Golf cones or colored string
- ✓ ParKit colored golf balls (4 of each color; 1 color per team)
- ✓ 1 ParKit Golf "Cow Ball"

Setup: Please refer to the drawing on the facing page.

- ➤ Make a boundary using 4 ParKit cones, colored string, or use the entire putting green.

- ➤ Distribute one ball of each color randomly within the boundaries. Place the cow ball somewhere within the boundaries.

How To Play:

- Create 2-4 teams (need not be equal size), or play individually. Each player or team is assigned a ball color and must stand outside the boundary behind their assigned cone until it is their turn.

- Select a player or team to go first. Play then continues in a clockwise direction. The order of play remains the same throughout the game.

- Each player putts one of their assigned colored balls. If the putt is holed, the player continues putting. If not, the player returns to their assigned cone, outside the boundaries. When all of a team's colored balls are holed, they may putt the cow ball.

- A player may also choose to knock another team's ball either toward or away from the hole by hitting it with his own ball. If the other ball is holed, the player may continue putting. If the other team's ball is knocked outside the boundaries, the ball is considered to be holed for the other team and the player loses his turn.

COW PASTURE POOL

- While a player is putting, any other player not standing at their assigned cone and outside the boundaries loses his next turn.

- No ball may be marked or otherwise moved during play, except by hitting it with another ball in the normal course of play.

- If a player holes the cow ball before holing all of his or her own colored balls, that player or team must skip one turn.

- The winner is the first team to hole all of their balls and the cow ball. The winner then gets one additional ball of their color added for the next round. The overall winner is the first player or team to win using all four of their own colored balls.

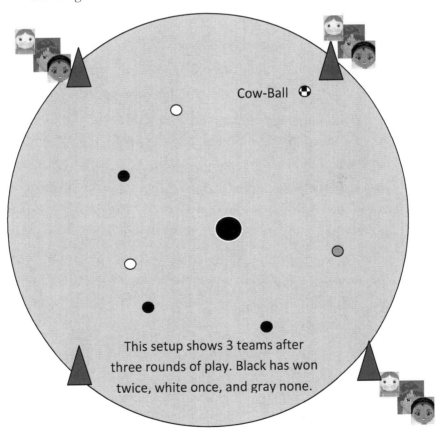

Cow-Ball

This setup shows 3 teams after three rounds of play. Black has won twice, white once, and gray none.

ESCAPE ARTIST

Overview: This game for 2 or more players helps develop:

✓ Advanced trouble shot skills for handling difficult lies anywhere around the green.

Equipment Required:

✓ 1-5 ParKit Golf cones
✓ 1 ParZone large ring

Setup: Please refer to the drawing on the facing page.

➤ Place six golf balls in difficult lies around the green such as in a bunker (e.g., "fried egg", buried, rake furrow, footprint, side hill, downhill, etc.), deep grass, near vegetation, on bare lies, on slopes, etc..

➤ Place one ParKit cone where players will await their turn.

➤ If the practice area is not near a green, place four ParKit cones in a rectangle, representing a green-sized target area for intermediate skill level players.

➤ Place the ParZone ring as a target for advanced skill level players.

How To Play:

• Determine the order of play among the players.

• Following the order of play, players will take turns attempting to hit a ball out of the difficult lies.

• The winner is the first player to get three balls out of the difficult lies and stopping the balls either within either the cones, on the green, or within the ParZone ring, depending on the skill level of the players.

• The instructor may optionally require the players to use two or more different clubs to hit the shots.

44

ESCAPE ARTIST

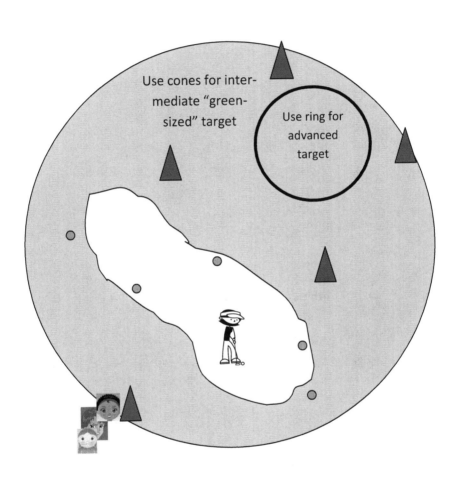

FLOPPER STOPPER

Overview: This game for 2-6 players helps to develop:

- ✓ Pitching distance control
- ✓ Flop shot technique

Equipment Required:

- ✓ 6 ParKit Golf cones
- ✓ 2 ParKit Golf aiming sticks
- ✓ ParKit Golf scoring pad
- ✓ ParKit Golf colored string

Setup: Please refer to the drawing on the facing page.

- ➤ Create a pitching station by placing 2 ParKit cones 6 feet apart in a flat area appropriate for pitching up to 40 yards.

- ➤ Place 1 ParKit cone where players will await their turn.

- ➤ Place 3 ParKit cones in a line approximately 20 feet away from the pitching station, close enough together so that the ParKit aiming sticks can be placed on top of the cones.

- ➤ Use the ParKit string to create a series of lines parallel to the above 3 cones, spaced every 5 paces from the cones. Assign point values to the spaces within the lines: 1st area is 100 points, 2nd area is 50 points; 3rd area is 10 points.

How To Play:

- ➤ The object of the game is to pitch or flop a ball over the cone and aiming stick barrier and make the ball stop as quickly as possible, scoring the most points.

- ➤ Decide on the order of play. Each player will line up behind the "on-deck" cone until it is their turn to pitch.

- ➤ Taking turns, each player will pitch 3 balls. The ball must fly over the cone/aiming stick barrier. The player scores points ac-

FLOPPER STOPPER

cording to where the ball comes to rest, using the point values for each space within the lines.

➤ The winner is the player with the most points after 3 rounds (the instructor may change the number of rounds).

➤ The instructor may change the spacing of the lines to make the point scoring areas larger or smaller as needed, depending on the skill level of the players.

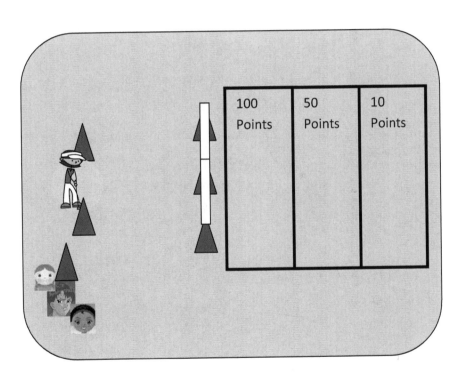

G-O-L-F

<u>Overview</u>: This game for 2 or more players helps develop:

✓ Full swing advanced shot shaping and ball control

Equipment Required:

✓ 3 ParKit Golf cones
✓ ParKit Golf scoring pad

<u>Setup</u>: Please refer to the drawing on the facing page.

➢ Make a full swing station by placing two ParKit cones about 6 feet apart on the practice tee suitable for full driver shots. Place a supply of golf balls in the station.

➢ Place one ParKit cone where players will await their turn.

How To Play:

• Determine the order of play among the players.

• Following the order of play, players will take turns following the directions of the instructor.

• The instructor will state what club the first player must use.

• The instructor will also describe the type of shot to hit (e.g., a hook, slice, straight, high, low, or medium trajectory shot).

• If the player does not successfully execute the required shot, he gets the next letter of the word "G-O-L-F", and the instructor selects the shot for the next player in line.

• If the player does successfully execute the required shot (to the satisfaction of the instructor), the player selects the type of shot for the next player in line.

• If that player does not successfully execute the shot, he gets a letter. If he does, he then selects the shot for the next player, and so on.

G-O-L-F

- When a player accumulates all of the letters G-O-L-F, he is out of the game.

- The winner is the last player remaining.

.

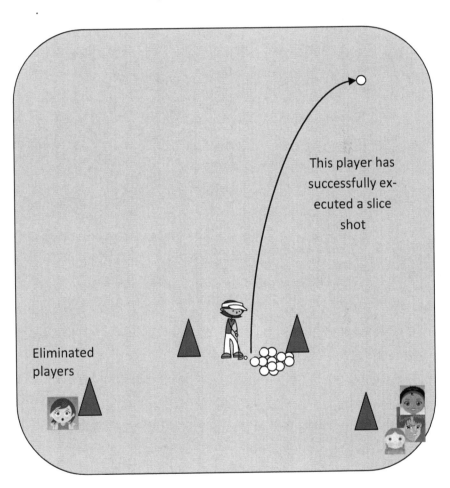

GOLFABULARY

Overview: Golfabulary is a pressure-packed golf knowledge and memory game for almost any number of players. An ideal indoor game, Golfabulary builds knowledge of the rules of golf, golf course features, golf club design, and general golf knowledge. It also rewards paying careful attention to others' answers and the ability to think quickly.

Golfabulary helps develop overall golf knowledge and etiquette.

Equipment Required:

✓ No special equipment is required.

Setup: No special setup is required. However, it is helpful to arrange all players in a line or in a circle around the instructor.

How To Play:

Beginning with the youngest or least experienced player, ask that player to say a golf word or phrase. The instructor should repeat the word or phrase so that all players can hear it. Going in order, the next player then must say a different golf word or phrase within 5 seconds. Each time, the instructor repeats the word or phrase to ensure that all players have heard it correctly.

If a player repeats a word or phrase that has already been said, that player is out (at the instructor's option, the player may get a second chance to say a unique golf word or phrase that has not already been said).

If a player is unable to think of a new golf word or phrase within the 5 second time limit, he or she is out (at the instructor's discretion, more time may be permitted).

The game continues going around from player to player until only two players are left. At that point, if one of the players is unable to think of a new golf word or phrase, the other player must do so within 5 seconds in order to win. If that player cannot do it, the other player gets another 5 seconds to say a new golf word or phrase. This continues until only one player remains.

GOLFABULARY

The following table includes examples of words that can be used in Golfabulary. Without a doubt, you will be able to think of many more.

Teeing ground	Lateral hazard	Flex	Penalty
Tee box	Water hazard	Hosel	Scorecard
Tee marker	Red stake	Neck	In
Tee	Yellow stake	Clubhead	Out
Fairway	White stake	Toe	Handicap
Rough	Out of bounds	Heel	Double-eagle
Green	Loose impediment	Sole	Eagle
Fringe	Moveable Obstruction	Sweet spot	Birdie
Frog Hair	Immoveable obstruction	Grooves	Par
Putting Surface	Unplayable lie	Face	Bogey
Hole	Lost ball	Wood	Double-bogey
Flagstick	Clublength	Iron	Triple-bogey
Flag	Drop	Hybrid	Putt
Cup	Lift	Putter	Drive
Hole liner	Place	Vardon	Slice
Bunker	Replace	Overlap	Hook
Rake	Clean	Interlock	Fade
Hazard	Golf club	Crosshand	Draw
Water	Grip	Match play	Top
Sand	Shaft	Stroke play	Shank

GOLF BINGO

Overview: Golf Bingo uses a special Golf Bingo scoresheet with letters of the alphabet and plays like regular bingo, but with a twist. That twist requires players to learn golf and rules terminology, and makes the game fun for any number of players in an indoor setting.

Equipment Required:

- ✓ ParKit Golf Bingo sheets
- ✓ Alphabet letter cards (one card for each letter of the alphabet)

Setup: No special setup is required. Refer to the sheet on the facing page for an example of a winning Golf Bingo sheet.

How To Play:

Give a Golf Bingo sheet and a pencil to each player. The instructor draws a letter card and announces it to the players. If a player's Golf Bingo card contains that letter, they may claim that square by writing a golf word or phrase that begins with the letter.

For example, if the letter is "T", a player may write "teeing ground" in the square and claim the "T".

When a player has claimed all squares in a row, column, or diagonal, he or she yells "Golf Bingo!" and must show his or her Golf Bingo sheet to the instructor for approval. If the golf words or phrases meet approval, the player wins the game. If not, that player is eliminated and the game continues until a winner is selected.

GOLF BINGO

Golf Bingo Sheet			
T *Teeing ground*	**B** *Ball*	**H** *Hole*	**F**
I	**G** *Grip*	**C** *Clubhead*	**P**
H	**U** *Unplayable lie*	**O**	**M**
S	**T** *Tee marker*	**E**	**H**

This player wins Golf Bingo by successfully writing golf words or phrases for each letter in the second column.

GOLF BOWLS

Overview: This game mimics Lawn Bowls or Bocce, and is excellent for pitching, chipping or putting. It may be played by 2 or more players or teams, and helps to develop:

- ✓ Direction and distance control
- ✓ Strategy

Equipment Required:

- ✓ 6 ParKit Golf cones
- ✓ ParKit Golf scoring pad
- ✓ 4 ParKit Golf colored golf balls for each team, plus 1 ParKit Golf black "8-ball".

Setup: Please refer to the drawing on the facing page.

- ➢ Create a chipping station by placing 2 ParKit cones 6 feet apart in a flat area appropriate for chipping up to 30 yards.

- ➢ Place 1-2 ParKit cones where players will await their turn.

- ➢ Place 2 ParKit cones 10 feet apart, 20 yards away from the chipping station to define the far end of the chipping area.

How To Play:

- ➢ Create two teams (need not be equal sized). Each team receives 4 golf balls of the team's color. Determine which team is to play first.

- ➢ Place the ParKit black "8-ball" within the chipping area to be used as the target ball (the "jack" in Bocce).

- ➢ Each team will determine their own order of play. Players wait behind the "on-deck" cone until it is their turn.

GOLF BOWLS

➤ A player from the starting team will hit one ball toward the jack, either putting, chipping, or pitching, depending on how the game is to be played. Then, the other team will hit a ball toward the jack.

➤ From then on, the team that does not have the ball closest to the jack will hit, until one team has used all 4 balls. At that point, the other team hits its remaining balls, one per player.

➤ A ball may strike any other ball or the jack, moving either one.

➤ The team with the closest ball to the jack is the only team that can score points. The scoring team receives one point for each of their balls that is closer to the jack than the closest ball of the other team. The winner is the first team to 7 points.

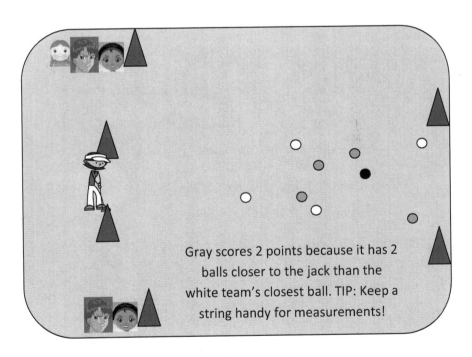

Gray scores 2 points because it has 2 balls closer to the jack than the white team's closest ball. TIP: Keep a string handy for measurements!

GOLF HANGMAN

Overview: Golf Hangman is a way to combine golf knowledge, spelling, and skills, and is a perfect indoor rainy day game.

Equipment Required:

✓ An easel with a large whiteboard and dry-erase markers. If a whiteboard is not available, large easel paper will work.

Setup: Please refer to the drawing on the facing page.

➢ Begin with a blank whiteboard and think of a golf word or phrase.

➢ Draw underline dashes to represent each letter in the word or phrase, but don't divulge the answer.

How To Play:

• Divide the players into two teams. Teams do not need to be of equal size, but they should have a similar mix of ages and golf knowledge.

• Beginning with one team, ask them to guess a letter that is a part of the word or phrase. If they guess correctly, write the letter above the underline dash. If not, write the letter below to show that it has been guessed but was not found in the word or phrase.

• If the team guesses correctly, they may try to solve the word or phrase. If not, the other team gets its turn to guess a letter.

• Continue until one team correctly guesses the word or phrase.

• The winning team gets a point.

GOLF HANGMAN

- Erase the board and start again with a new word or phrase.

- The first team to win three points is the champion of Golf Hangman.

A team correctly guessed the word "golf." However, the letters "e", "h", and "a" were also guessed but were incorrect.

GOLF LADDER

<u>Overview</u>: This game for 2 or more players helps develop:

- ✓ Chip, pitch, or bunker shot direction and distance control.

Equipment Required:

- ✓ 3 ParKit Golf cones
- ✓ 6 ParKit Golf aiming sticks
- ✓ ParKit Golf scoring pad

<u>Setup</u>: Please refer to the drawing on the facing page.

➢ Make a hitting station by placing two ParKit cones about 6 feet apart in the bunker. Place a supply of golf balls in the station.

➢ Place one ParKit cone where players will await their turn.

➢ Beginning about 5 yards from the bunker, insert one ParKit aiming stick into the ground. Moving in a zig-zag pattern, insert the remaining aiming sticks in 5 yard increments moving away from the hitting station (see drawing of bunker shot example).

How To Play:

- Determine the order of play among the players.

- Following the order of play, players will take turns attempting to hit a ball toward one of the aiming sticks that the instructor has designated for each round.

- Players receive points based on their rank order proximity to the designated aiming stick. For example, if there are 5 players, the player closest to the aiming stick receives 5 points; the next closest receives 4 points, etc., and the farthest away receives 1 point.

- Every player receives 1 point for trying, regardless of proximity to the aiming stick.

GOLF LADDER

- Players must keep track of their own point total after each round.

- The winner is the player with the most points after six rounds (one round for each aiming stick "ladder rung").

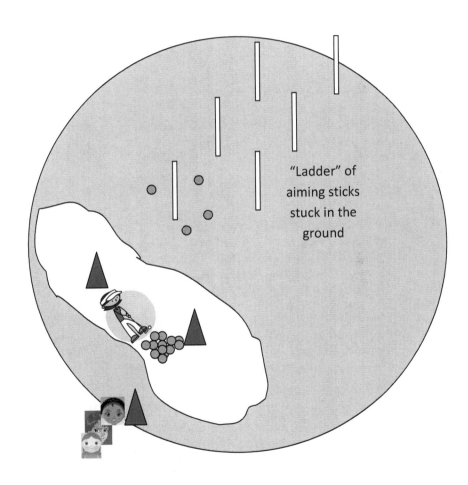

"Ladder" of aiming sticks stuck in the ground

HOME RUN DERBY

<u>Overview</u>: This team game helps develop:

- ✓ Consistency in hitting full shots
- ✓ Performance under pressure

Equipment Required:

- ✓ 6 ParKit Golf cones
- ✓ 4 ParKit Golf aiming sticks
- ✓ ParKit Golf scoring pad

<u>Setup</u>: Please refer to the drawing on the facing page.

➢ Make a full swing station by aligning two ParKit aiming sticks about 6 feet apart on the practice tee suitable for full driver shots. Place a supply of golf balls in the station.

➢ Place one ParKit cone for each team, where players will await their turn.

➢ Create a "home run fence" by using two ParKit aiming sticks for the left and right field foul poles and arranging four ParKit cones to represent the outfield fence. The instructor should use judgment in deciding how far away the "fence" should be.

How To Play:

- Create two teams (need not be equal sized). Determine which team is to play first. Each team will determine its "batting order". Players wait behind their "on-deck" cone until it is their turn.

- Decide in advance how many "innings" will be played.

- Taking turns, the teams "come to bat" following their team "batting order". Each player attempts to hit a ball over the "fence" in the air. If successful, one "run" is scored.

- If the ball does not clear the "fence" or is a "foul ball" (outside the aiming stick "foul poles", the team gets an "out". After 3 "outs", the "inning" is over and the other team "comes to bat".

HOME RUN DERBY

- The winner is the team with the most runs after the agreed-upon number of innings.

KING OF THE BUNKER

Overview: This game for 2 or more players helps develop:

- ✓ Bunker shot direction and distance control.

Equipment Required:

- ✓ 3 ParKit Golf cones
- ✓ 3 ParKit Golf rings (small, medium, large)

Setup: Please refer to the drawing on the facing page.

- ➤ Make a bunker station by placing two ParKit cones about 6 feet apart in the bunker. Place a supply of golf balls in the station.

- ➤ Place one ParKit cone where players will await their turn.

- ➤ Place three ParZone rings at increasing distances from the bunker, beginning with the smallest ring, then the medium ring, then the large ring (use your judgment on distances from the bunker).

How To Play:

- • Determine the order of play among the players.

- • Following the order of play, players will take turns attempting to hit a ball out of the bunker into each of the rings.

- • In order to win the game, a player must hit, in any order, one ball anywhere out of the bunker, and one ball into each of the rings.

- • The winner is the first player to complete all four requirements.

- • For lesser skilled players, the game may be modified by using only the largest rings. Alternatively, only one or two rings may be used to simplify the game.

KING OF THE BUNKER

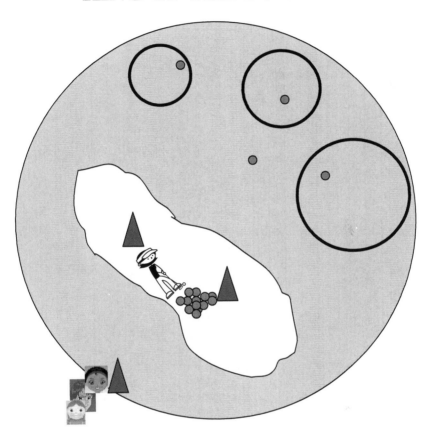

KNOCKOUT

Overview: This team game helps to develop:

- ✓ Overall putting skills
- ✓ Performance under pressure
- ✓ Decision-making strategy

Equipment Required:

- ✓ 4 ParKit Golf cones
- ✓ 2 ParKit Golf aiming sticks
- ✓ 2 ParKit Golf ball markers

Setup: Please refer to the drawing on the facing page.

- ➤ Place the ParKit ball markers approximately 1 foot apart and 6-8 feet from a hole on the putting green.

- ➤ Place 1 ParKit aiming stick on each side of the ball markers, about 6 feet away where players will await their turn.

- ➤ Away from the hole, place the 4 ParKit cones in a rectangle to be used as a "penalty box".

How To Play:

- Create 2 teams (need not be equal size) and direct each team's players to stand in order behind one of the ParKit aiming sticks. Determine which team will go first. The teams will alternate taking turns. Each team should determine its own order of play.

- Each player will place his ball between the ball markers and putt. If the putt is holed, the player may either:

  1. Choose a player from the other team to go to the penalty box, or

  2. Choose a player from his own team to come back from the penalty box. That player will then putt first on the team's next turn.

KNOCKOUT

- A player may not be sent to the penalty box for a second time until all of his teammates have also been sent there at least once.

- Once a player has been sent to the penalty box twice, he may not be brought back into the game.

- A team wins when all players from the other team are in the penalty box.

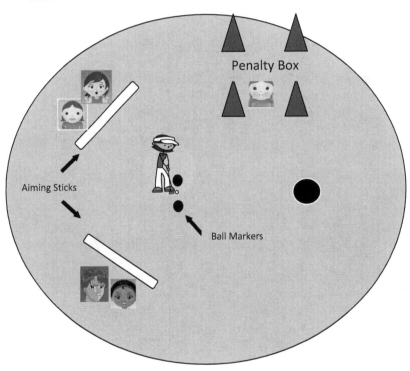

LAGMASTER

Overview: LagMaster is a putting distance control game that focuses on both long and short putts. The object is to hole each ball in the fewest strokes possible.

Equipment Required:

- ✓ 5 balls
- ✓ 4 ball markers or tees
- ✓ 6' ParZone ring

Setup: Please refer to the drawing on the facing page.

➤ Place the 6' ParZone ring around a hole on the putting green as shown.

➤ Place the ball markers 5 feet, 10 feet, 20 feet, and 40 feet from the hole.

How To Play:

➤ Beginning with all 5 balls at the 40' marker, putt each ball toward the hole surrounded by the ParZone target ring, counting each stroke.

➤ Any ball that is holed is removed from future play.

➤ Any ball that finishes within the ParZone target ring is moved to the next closest marker.

➤ Continue putting the remaining balls from the same marker until each ball is either holed or finishes within the ParZone target ring. Remember to count each stroke.

➤ When all remaining balls have reached the closest marker (the 5' marker), remove the ParZone ring and putt the remaining balls to the hole until all of the balls are holed, continuing to count each stroke.

LAGMASTER

➢ The game is over when all 5 balls have been holed from any distance.

➢ Keep a record of the number of putts you require to hole all five balls and attempt to set a new (lower) record each time you play.

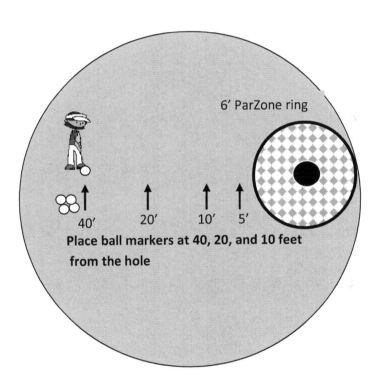

6' ParZone ring

40'   20'   10'   5'

Place ball markers at 40, 20, and 10 feet from the hole

LANDING ZONE

Overview: Landing Zone helps develop distance and directional control for short game shots. When hitting shots from around the green, focus on where the ball should land in order to roll to the hole. The object is to land the ball in the correct spot for chipping, pitching, and bunker shots.

Equipment Required:

✓   3' and 6' ParZone rings
✓   2 ball markers

Setup: Please refer to the drawing on the facing page.

➤   Place 2 ball markers or tees 6 feet apart in an area suitable for chipping, pitching or bunker shots of any length. Many setups are possible, depending on whether you are playing the game while chipping, pitching, or hitting bunker shots. Place a supply of golf balls in the station.

➤   Place the 3' or 6' ParZone ring on the green or another suitable landing place. Try to determine where the ball should land in order to roll to your target (the hole or other target).

How To Play:

➤   The object of the game is to land your ball inside the ParZone target ring as many times in a row as possible.

➤   Keep a record of the number of times in a row you are able to land a ball inside the ParZone target ring, and attempt to set a new record each time you play the game.

➤   Practice using different clubs while chipping or pitching, continuing to land the ball within the ParZone target ring. Pay close attention to where the ball ends up with different clubs.

LANDING ZONE

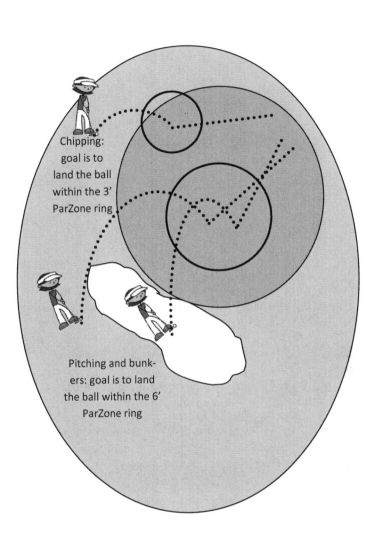

Chipping: goal is to land the ball within the 3' ParZone ring

Pitching and bunkers: goal is to land the ball within the 6' ParZone ring

LAST ONE STANDING

Overview: This game of elimination tests the students':

- ✓ Distance control
- ✓ Ability to focus amid time limits and distractions
- ✓ Ability to remember and follow directions

Equipment Required:

- ✓ 2-5 ParKit Golf cones
- ✓ Colored string (25 feet or more)
- ✓ ParKit Golf scoring pad
- ✓ Each player needs his own ball, marked for identification

Setup: Please refer to the drawing on the facing page.

➢ Stretch string across one side of the putting green. Place 2 Par-Kit cones approximately 25 feet away from the string.

➢ If space permits and teams are used, another set of cones may be placed equidistant from the string on the opposite side from the other cones (as shown in the drawing).

How To Play:

- Create two teams (need not be equal size), or play individually. All players line up between the cones, aiming toward the line. If teams are used, they may line up on opposite sides of the string.

- The instructor will announce "3-2-1… PUTT!", and all players will putt toward the string at the same time. Anyone putting early or late (in instructor's judgment) is eliminated from the round.

- The farthest ball from the string is out, and that player is eliminated (more than one may be eliminated to speed play).

- If teams are used, the teams switch sides for the next round.

- Players must not leave their putting spot until it has been determined who will be eliminated. Any player who leaves early to

LAST ONE STANDING

retrieve his ball is eliminated in addition to the one farthest from the line.

- The winner is the last player standing.

- Variation: In team play, rather than eliminating a player, the player with the ball *closest* to the string wins a point for the team. Use the ParKit Scoring Pad to keep score. The winner is the first team to reach 10 points.

- Variation: The player closest to the line may choose a player from the other team to be eliminated. When all players for a team are eliminated, the other team wins.

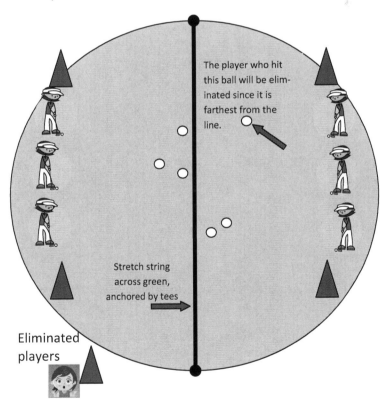

The player who hit this ball will be eliminated since it is farthest from the line.

Stretch string across green, anchored by tees

Eliminated players

LINE IT UP

Overview: Line It Up helps focus on putting directional control by helping you learn to roll the ball in a perfectly straight line. Line It Up is also friendly for greenskeepers who do not like chalk putting lines on the green.

Equipment Required:

- ✓ 5 golf balls
- ✓ ParKit Golf putting pins and string

Setup: Please refer to the drawing on the facing page.

- ➢ Find a flat portion of the putting green where you will have a straight putt. You can find a straight putt on a sloped green by making a few test rolls to the hole from different locations.

- ➢ Tie a 10 foot length of string to the pins and push one putting pin into the green about 3 inchesbehind the hole.

- ➢ Push the other putting pin into the green about 10 feet from the hole at the spot from which you will have a straight putt and tighten so that the string is taut. The string should be a few inches off the green.

How To Play:

- ➢ Place a ball directly under the string. Paying attention to the path of your club head compared to the string, putt the ball toward the hole. The ball should stay on line with the string. Continue putting until you miss, scoring a point for each holed putt.

- ➢ Keep a record of the number of points you score, and attempt to set a new record each time you play the game.

LINE IT UP

> ➤ If competing with multiple players, the winner is the player with the most points, once all players have had an equal number of turns.

Taut string tied to
each putting pin

Straight putt

Ball should follow
string line to hole

MONUMENTAL

Overview: Monumental helps develop long putting skills, emphasizing both distance control and accuracy.

Equipment Required:

- ✓ 1 roll of ParKit string
- ✓ Tees
- ✓ ParKit colored golf balls, or regular golf balls.

Setup: Please refer to the drawing on the facing page.

➤ Locate an area where the green is level, providing for a straight putt from about 30 feet away from a hole.

➤ Beginning about 30 feet from the hole, stretch a string until it is about two feet past the hole and about 6 inches left of the hole. Secure the string with a tee stuck into the green.

➤ Stretch the string 1 more foot to make a point 3 feet directly behind the hole.

➤ Mirror the design on the right side of the hole, ending directly across from where you began.

➤ Insert four pairs of tees or ParKit markers on either side of the string in one-foot increments away from the hole.

How To Play:

- Create teams or play individually.

- Each player gets five attempts to putt a ball within the string toward the hole. The ball must come to rest within the string in order to score points.

- Remove each ball from the playing area after it comes to rest, so that it does not interfere with the play of subsequent balls.

MONUMENTAL

- Score points as follows:

  o One point if the ball comes to rest past the first set of tees.
  o Two points if the ball comes to rest past the second set of tees.
  o Three points if the ball comes to rest past the third set of tees.
  o Four points if the ball comes to rest past the fourth set of tees.
  o Five points if the ball comes to rest past the hole.
  o Ten points if the ball is holed.

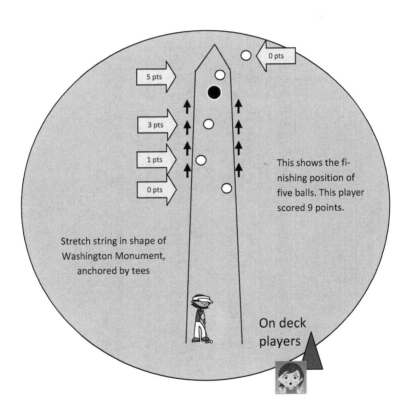

5 pts

3 pts

1 pts

0 pts

0 pts

This shows the finishing position of five balls. This player scored 9 points.

Stretch string in shape of Washington Monument, anchored by tees

On deck players

PINK PLANK PLUNK

Overview: Pink Plank Plunk is a game of short putting skill. Actually, it isn't just one game, but there are many ways to use the Pink Plank™ to improve your short putting skills. When the Pink Plank is on the green, everyone wants to give it a try.

Equipment Required:

✓ ParKit Pink Plank

Setup: Please refer to the drawing on the facing page.

➢ Find a level spot on the putting green so that the Pink Plank will lay flat and level (especially from side to side), with the "100" point end about 3 inches from the hole. Test the location by rolling a ball along the Pink Plank to see if it tends to curve off to one side or.the other. If the ball tends to fall off, move the far end of the Pink Plank toward that side, keeping the "100" point end aimed at the hole and try rolling the ball again.

➢ When set up correctly, a ball will roll along the Pink Plank and go "Plunk" into the hole!

How To Play:

The object is to putt a ball along the Pink Plank so that it rolls all the way to the hole and goes "Plunk." Beginners may start closer to the hole, earning more points the farther down the Pink Plank their ball goes before falling off.

More experienced players should begin at the starting dot and try to hole as many putts in a row as possible.

PINK PLANK PLUNK

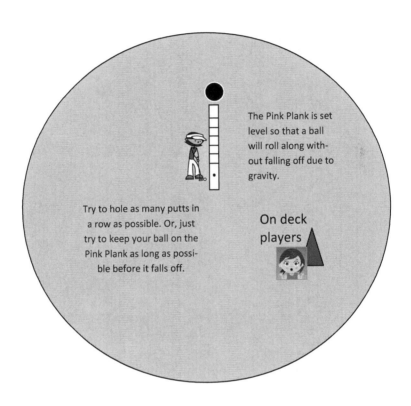

The Pink Plank is set level so that a ball will roll along without falling off due to gravity.

Try to hole as many putts in a row as possible. Or, just try to keep your ball on the Pink Plank as long as possible before it falls off.

On deck players

POLE VAULT

Overview: This game for 1 or more players helps to develop:

- ✓ Pitching or flop shot technique

Equipment Required:

- ✓ 4 ParKit Golf cones
- ✓ 4 ParKit Golf aiming sticks
- ✓ 1 Foam pool noodle

Setup: Please refer to the drawing on the facing page.

- ➢ Create a pitching station by placing 2 ParKit cones 6 feet apart in a flat area appropriate for pitching up to 40 yards.

- ➢ Place 1 ParKit cone where players will await their turn.

- ➢ Place the final ParKit cone where players will go when eliminated from the game.

- ➢ Assemble a "pole vault high bar" by connecting two or more pairs of aiming sticks, and push each set of sticks into the ground six feet apart until they are stable. Then, attach the pool noodle to the top of each pair of aiming sticks.

How To Play:

- ➢ The object of the game is to pitch or flop a ball over the pole vault high bar.

- ➢ Decide on the order of play. Each player will line up behind the "on-deck" cone until it is their turn to pitch.

- ➢ Taking turns, each player will attempt to pitch a ball over the high bar. If successful, that player advances to the next round. If not, that player is eliminated.

POLE VAULT

➢ After the round is complete, if 2 or more players remain in the game, the tee marker cones are moved closer to the high bar, and the players again attempt to pitch a ball over the bar.

➢ The winner is the player who successfully pitches a ball over the high bar from the closest point to the bar. If neither player is successful, additional rounds may be played until only one player succeeds in clearing the high bar.

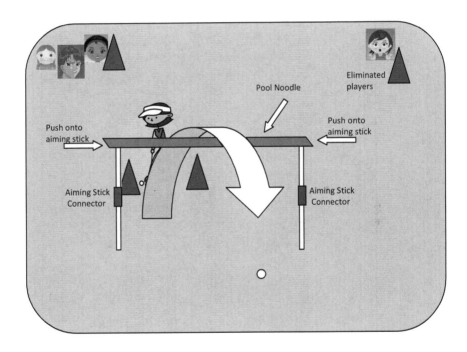

PRESSURE COOKER

Overview: This game for two or more players helps develop:

- ✓ Consistent full swing shotmaking technique
- ✓ Performance under pressure

Equipment Required:

- ✓ 5 ParKit Golf cones
- ✓ 2 ParKit Golf aiming sticks
- ✓ ParKit Golf scoring pad

Setup: Please refer to the drawing on the facing page.

➢ Make a full swing station by aligning two ParKit aiming sticks about 6 feet apart on the practice tee suitable for full shots. Place a supply of golf balls in the station.

➢ Place one ParKit cone where players will await their turn.

➢ Place four ParKit cones in a rectangular shape on the range or hitting area a suitable distance from the hitting station, depending upon the club to be used for full shots and the skill level of the players. These cones will be used to define the target area for full shots, so place them defining a large target area such as a green or fairway (see drawing).

How To Play:

- Determine the order of play. Players wait behind the "on-deck" cone until it is their turn.

- Define the goal for the players as a shot that lands within the target area marked by the four cones.

- Following the order of play, each player will take a turn hitting shots toward the target area. If the player's ball lands within the target area, he scores one point and continues until he hits a ball that does not land within the target area.

PRESSURE COOKER

- Each ball that scores a goal counts as one point. The player's turn ends when he fails to score.

- The winner is the player who scores the most points after everyone has had an equal number of turns.

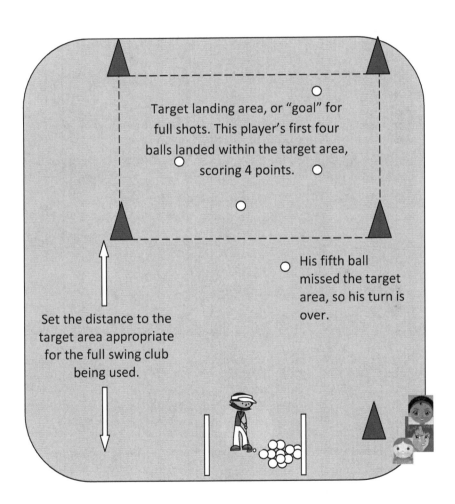

Target landing area, or "goal" for full shots. This player's first four balls landed within the target area, scoring 4 points.

His fifth ball missed the target area, so his turn is over.

Set the distance to the target area appropriate for the full swing club being used.

PUTT N' SPIN

Overview: Putt n' Spin is a putting game of skill and chance, and it really makes the player focus on each putt and try to do his or her best each time… or else.

Equipment Required:

- ✓ ParKit Putt n' Spin spinner
- ✓ Four colored balls: Orange, Green, Yellow, and Blue.

Setup: No special setup is required, other than space on the putting green.

How To Play:

- Choose a starting point for putting to a hole. The putt can be of any length and level of difficulty, depending on the skill level of the players. Place a tee marker in the green at that point.

- Begin by putting one of the colored balls toward the hole. The goal is to make the putt, so try your best each time.

- Continue putting each colored ball. If a ball blocks the hole, or if you want to eliminate the possibility of a ball striking another ball, mark each ball after each putt.

- Once all four colored balls have been putted, spin the ParKit Putt n' Spin spinner to see which ball will count.

- There are several ways to use the spinner. You may use the colors to select the ball to count. Pick up the other balls and mark the position of the ball of the color pointed to by the spinner.

- If the spinner points to "spin again," spin again and follow the words to select which ball will count. Or, continue using the colors

PUTT N' SPIN

(decide which method you will use ahead of time).

- Place all four colored balls near the mark of the selected ball and continue as above, putting each ball.

- If each ball is holed, there is no need to spin – your ball is holed. If not, you must spin the spinner to see which ball will count.

- Keep your score as normal, counting each selected ball as one stroke.

Variations: The Putt n' Spin spinner may be incorporated into many other putting games, adding more fun and excitement to each game by introducing the element of chance.

RELAY RACE

Overview: This team game helps develop:

- ✓ Instinctive shotmaking, without becoming preoccupied with technique

Equipment Required:

- ✓ 5 ParKit Golf cones
- ✓ ParKit Golf scoring pad

Setup: Please refer to the drawing on the facing page.

- ➤ Make two bunker stations by placing two ParKit cones in the bunker, spaced far enough apart to allow two players to safely hit shots simultaneously. Next to each cone, place 8 golf balls.

- ➤ Place the other two ParKit cones out of the bunker where each team will await its turn.

- ➤ Place the final ParKit cone as an aiming aid for the players.

How To Play:

- Create two teams (need not be equal sized). Determine which team is to play first. Each team will determine its own order of play. Players wait behind the "on-deck" cone until it is their turn.

- Make sure it is clear which team is to use which bunker station.

- When the instructor says "GO", player #1 from each team runs into the bunker to hit a ball. Each player gets two attempts to hit one ball out of the bunker toward the aiming cone. If the player fails to hit the ball out, the player must throw it out of the bunker.

- Once the ball is out of the bunker, the player will run back to his team and tag the next player. This player will hit the next ball and the rotation will continue until one team has no balls remaining.

- When one team's balls are all out of the bunker, that team wins the round and scores one point.

RELAY RACE

- The teams then return to their respective on-deck cones and the instructor resets the bunker stations with eight golf balls for the next round.

- The winner is the first team to reach 5 points.

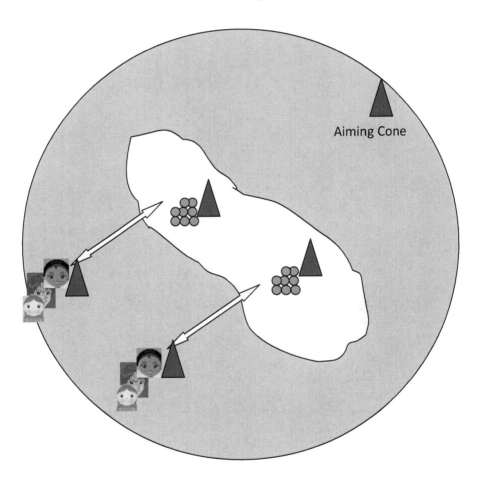

Aiming Cone

RINGER

Overview: This game for two or more people plays like the popular "marbles" game, and helps develop:

- ✓ Directional control
- ✓ Distance control
- ✓ Game strategy

Equipment Required:

- ✓ 4 white golf balls for each player, plus 1 additional white ball
- ✓ 1 colored ball for each player
- ✓ 6' ParZone ring

Setup: Please refer to the drawing on the facing page.

- ➢ Place the ParZone target ring on the putting green, away from a hole.

- ➢ Arrange the white balls in a "+" shape, as shown.

- ➢ Each player may place their own colored ball on an inside edge of the ParZone target ring.

How To Play:

- Determine the order of play.

- The object of the game is to knock the white balls out of the ParZone ring by putting the colored ball into a white ball, causing the white ball to roll out of the ring.

- If a player knocks one or more white balls out of the ParZone ring, that player claims those white balls continues putting.

- If the player fails to knock a white ball out of the ParZone target ring, the player's turn ends.

- If the player's colored ball goes out of the ParZone target ring, the player's turn ends and the colored ball is placed on the inside edge of the ring where it last crossed.

RINGER

- If a player knocks another player's colored ball out of the ParZone target ring, the player's turn ends. The player whose ball was knocked out may place the other player's ball anywhere on an inside edge of the ring, and may place their own ball anywhere within the ParZone rings for their next putt.

- The winner is the player with the most white balls, once all white balls have been knocked out of the ParZone ring. If two players tie with the most white balls, the first player to reach that number is the winner.

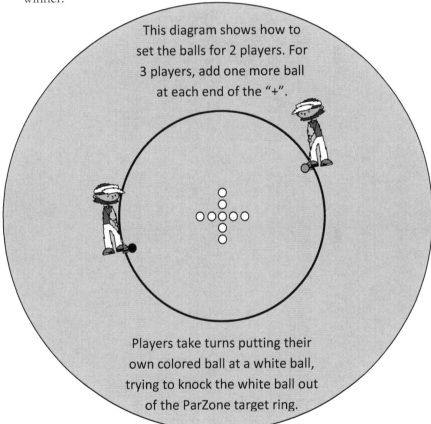

This diagram shows how to set the balls for 2 players. For 3 players, add one more ball at each end of the "+".

Players take turns putting their own colored ball at a white ball, trying to knock the white ball out of the ParZone target ring.

RULES O'FISHLE

Overview: Rules O'Fishle is a game of golf knowledge, chance, and skill, and is great for indoors or outdoors. There are many ways to play the game, and you can use your imagination to create dozens of fun variations from this basic example.

Equipment Required:

- ✓ ParKit golf rules flashcards, or your own rules questions.
- ✓ A whiteboard, large paper sheet, or poster board and appropriate marking pens.
- ✓ Small game tokens – one for each player or team.
- ✓ The ParKit Pink Plank, or other way of measuring golf skill
- ✓ One golf ball and putter, or each player may use their own putter.

Setup: Please refer to the drawing on the facing page.

➤ Prepare the whiteboard or poster by drawing a bird's-eye view of a golf hole as shown. Draw lines across the hole to use like spaces on a game board.

➤ Set the game tokens at the teeing ground.

➤ Arrange the rules cards or questions (sort by degree of difficulty or otherwise ensure they are appropriate for the skill and knowledge level of the players).

➤ Group the players into teams, or play individually if there are no more than five players.

How To Play:

Decide which team of player goes first, and have them draw a rules card. The team or player has the option to either answer the question or to pass it to the next team or player. If the team gets the correct answer, they get to putt on the Pink Plank. One representative from the team putts to determine how the team's token will move (players take turns

RULES O'FISHLE

putting so that all members of a team get a chance).

The farther the player's ball travels along the Pink Plank, the farther the team's token moves on the game board.

The first team whose token reaches the hole is the winner.

A 3-player game of Rules O'Fishle with 3 tokens on the board. The first player answered the rules question correctly and has putted on the Pink Plank, moving her token 7 spaces up the fairway.

SCHOOL

Overview: School is a ladder putting drill that helps develop distance control. The object is to roll the ball either into the hole or so that it stops within a close distance just past he hole. If successful, you "graduate" to the next grade and try again from farther away.

Equipment Required:

✓ 5 or more ball markers (either coins or tees work well)
✓ 3-foot ParZone ring

Setup: Please refer to the drawing on the facing page.

➢ Create a "passing zone" by placing the 3-foot ParZone ring around the hole as shown. The passing zone begins at the hole and includes the area within the ParZone target ring.

➢ Beginning a short distance from the hole, place the ball markers at 3-foot increments moving away from the hole. Use your judgment on the spacing of the markers. For beginners, keep the markers closer together. For advanced players, spread them farther apart.

➢ The closest marker represents "1st grade", the next marker "2nd grade", then "3rd grade", and so on.

How To Play:

➢ Beginning at "1st grade," putt toward the hole.

➢ If the ball is holed or finishes inside the "passing zone" the player advances to the next grade and putts again.

➢ If the ball does not finish either in the hole or within the passing zone, the player goes back to 1st grade.

➢ If it becomes too easy to reach the highest grade, spread the grade markers farther apart or use a breaking putt.

SCHOOL

➢ If playing individually, keep a record of the number of putts you require to reach the highest grade and attempt to set a new (lower) record each time you play.

➢ If competing with multiple players, the winner is the only player to reach the highest grade, once all players have had an equal number of turns (i.e., when a player reaches the end, any remaining players after him in the round get a chance to tie). In the event of a tie, continue adding grades farther from the hole until only one person passes. Another way to break a tie is to have the players continue to putt from the farthest grade until one "passes" and the other doesn't.

➢ The game may be made more challenging by using the smaller 1-foot diameter ParZone ring or by spacing the markers farther from the hole.

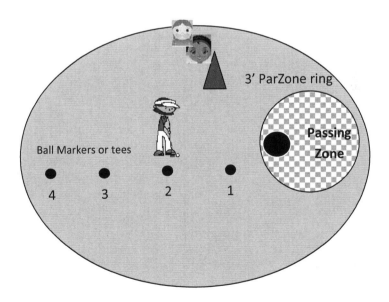

SCORECARD RACE

Overview: Scorecard Race is a multi-player version of Sequence that adds a new dimension of competition and pressure, simulating the pressure of real tournament golf. Scorecard Race challenges players to hit solid shots on target in order to win the race. As with real golf, there is a lot of pressure to hit great shots. Best of all, players will get really good at concentrating and focusing on the target

Equipment Required:

- ✓ Supply of practice balls
- ✓ Regular golf course scorecard
- ✓ Target (either a defined area, a practice green, or ParZone ring, depending upon the situation

Setup: Please refer to the drawing on the facing page.

➤ Using a regular scorecard, write the players' names on each line.

➤ Create a starting point by placing 2 ball markers or tees 6 feet apart either on the green (for putting) or in an area suitable for chipping, pitching or bunker shots of any length. Many setups are possible, depending on whether you are playing the game while putting, chipping, pitching, bunker, or full shots.

➤ Depending on whether you are playing Scorecard Race with putting, chipping, pitching, bunker, or full shots, you must create a target goal. This could be the hole, any size ring, or a even a practice green, depending upon your standard of an acceptable shot. For example, the target for a 3-foot putt would be the hole. The target for a long putt could be the 18" ParZone ring. Longer putts could use the 3' ParZone ring. Chips, pitch or bunker shots could use the 6' ParZone ring. Approach shots could use the 12' ParZone ring. Longer shots could use the entire green. If there is no practice green to use as a target for long shots, you can get creative and imagine a green-sized area any distance away. The goal should be set so that it is challenging, but still reasonably achievable.

SCORECARD RACE

How To Play:

The object of Scorecard Race is to be the first one to complete your scorecard by successfully hitting consecutive balls on the target.

Players take turns hitting one shot to the target and keeping score as follows. The first time you hit the target, put a mark in the scorecard box for hole number one. Each time your ball hits the target, you put a mark on your scorecard in the box for the next hole. If you miss the target, no mark.

The first person to put a mark in all nine boxes for the front nine of the scorecard is the winner, but the game doesn't end until each player has had the same number of turns.

If there is a tie after all players have had an equal number of turns, play continues with an elimination playoff. Continuing in the same order, those players who are tied take turns hitting to the target. If one player succeeds, any player who fails to hit the target is eliminated. Continue taking turns until only one player remains – the winner of the race.

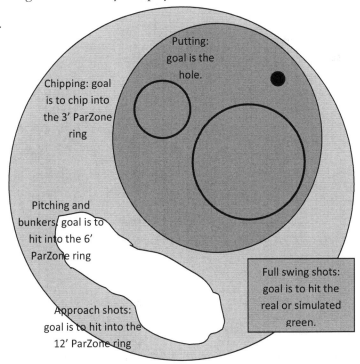

SCRAMBLED EGGS

Overview: Scrambled Eggs is a competitive game for two or more players that really tests their short game and putting skills. Scrambled Eggs plays like a typical scramble format, but with a "hard way" twist.

Equipment Required:

- ✓ 3 golf balls for each player
- ✓ Chipping or pitching club and putter

Setup: Please refer to the drawing on the facing page.

- ➤ Players take turns choosing a starting location for a chip or pitch shot around the green.

How To Play:

Easy Way: Each player hits three balls from the starting location using the club of their choice. The player then decides which shot will count, and the player's other two balls are picked up and moved to that location. The player cannot select a ball that is in the hole unless all three balls are holed. Each turn hitting three balls counts as one stroke. This process continues until each player has holed all three balls. The first player to win three times is the champion.

Hard Way: Each player hits three balls from the starting location using the club of their choice. The **opponents** must then decide which of the player's three shots will count, and the player's other two balls are picked up and moved to that location. Each turn hitting three balls counts as one stroke. This process continues until each player has holed all three balls. The first player to win three times is the champion.

SCRAMBLED EGGS

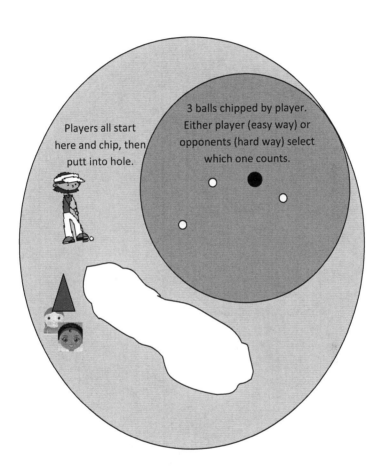

3 balls chipped by player. Either player (easy way) or opponents (hard way) select which one counts.

Players all start here and chip, then putt into hole.

SEQUENCE

Overview: A practice game for one person, Sequence tests your ability to repeatedly hit good shots with any club, and helps develop consistent shotmaking technique and performance under pressure.

Equipment Required:

- ✓ Supply of golf balls (either regular balls or range balls)
- ✓ ParZone ring (size determined by skill level)
- ✓ 2 ball markers or tees

Setup: Please refer to the drawing on the facing page.

➢ Create a starting point by placing 2 ball markers or tees 6 feet apart either on the green (for putting) or in an area suitable for chipping, pitching or bunker shots of any length. Many setups are possible, depending on whether you are playing the game while putting, chipping, pitching, bunker, or full shots.

➢ Depending on whether you are playing Sequence with putting, chipping, pitching, bunker, or full shots, you must create a target goal. This could be the hole, any size ring, or a even a practice green, depending upon your personal standard of an acceptable shot. The goal should be set so that it is challenging, but still reasonably achievable.

How To Play:

➢ The object of the game is to hit as many consecutive balls into your target as possible.

➢ Define your goal for the situation. For shorter putts, it might be the hole. For longer putts, it may be to putt the ball into the 3' ParZone ring. For chip, pitch, or standard bunker shots, it may be to stop the ball within the 6' ParZone ring. For difficult bunker shots, it may be to stop the ball on the green.

SEQUENCE

➢ Begin hitting shots toward your goal. If you succeed (as defined above), continue until you fail to achieve your goal.

➢ Each ball that scores a goal counts as one point. The game (or your turn) ends when you fail to score a goal.

➢ Keep a record of the number of points you score, and attemptt to set a new record each time you play the game.

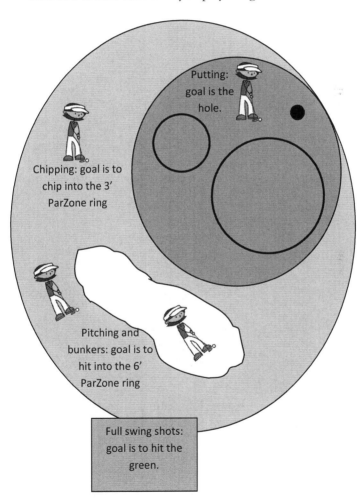

Putting: goal is the hole.

Chipping: goal is to chip into the 3' ParZone ring

Pitching and bunkers: goal is to hit into the 6' ParZone ring

Full swing shots: goal is to hit the green.

SHOOTOUT

Overview: This elimination game for 2 or more players helps develop:

- ✓ Pitching technique
- ✓ Direction and distance control
- ✓ Etiquette in order of play
- ✓ Strategy in approaching shots from different angles and situations

Equipment Required:

- ✓ 6 ParKit Golf cones
- ✓ ParKit Golf scoring pad

Setup: Please refer to the drawing on the facing page.

- ➢ Place the ParKit cones in six different locations around the practice green. Try to select locations that represent typical and challenging pitch or flop shot situations that a player may experience on the course.

How To Play:

- Determine the order of play among the players.

- Beginning at one of the ParKit cones, each player hits one shot toward the hole.

- Assign points to each player based on their ball's distance from the hole. The farthest away gets one point, the next closest gets 2 points, etc. If there are four players, the closest gets 4 points. Keep each player's point tally on the ParKit scoring pad.

- All players then move to the next ParKit cone for the next round, and scoring continues until all players have hit from each cone.

- The winner is the player with the most points after all players have played from each cone. Ties may be broken by a final shootout from one of the cones, with the closest player to the hole being the winner.

SHOOTOUT

- If desired, the instructor may choose to use fewer than six pitching locations.

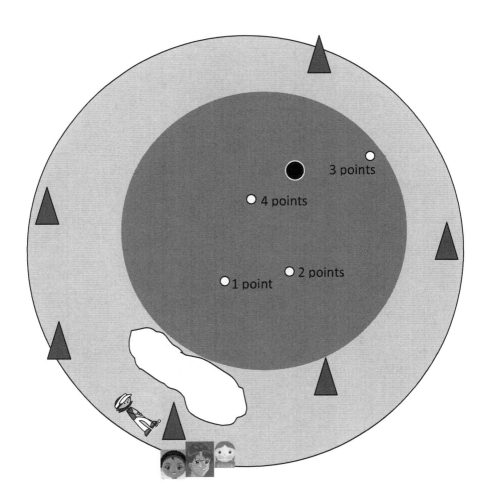

SLALOM COURSE

Overview: Slalom Course is great for non-golf course situations, and can be played on any open area. Slalom Course helps build golf hand-eye coordination and ball control, and is perfect for kids of any age.

Equipment Required:

- ✓ 3-5 ParKit aiming sticks with flags
- ✓ 2 ParKit cones
- ✓ Timing device (stopwatch, watch, or handheld device)
- ✓ 1 ball (either a golf ball, a foam ball, a mini-soccer ball, or a 6" beach ball)
- ✓ 1 club (can be a real golf club or a soft/plastic club for very young kids)

Setup: Please refer to the drawing on the facing page.

➢ Using an open area of a field or golf course, place 3-5 aiming sticks in the ground in a line as shown. Use ParKit flags on each aiming stick.

➢ Create a starting point by placing 2 ParKit cones as tee markers.

How To Play:

Taking turns or in teams, players begin by placing their ball behind the tee markers (cones). When the instructor says "go," the player runs the slalom course by hitting his or her ball around each aiming stick, as with slalom skiing. At the instructor's discretion, the players may hit their ball while running (like hockey), or they must come to a complete stop, take their stance, and then hit their ball.

There are two ways to determine the winner. First is by time, where the player who navigates the slalom course and crosses the start/finish line in the fastest time is the winner. Second is by number of strokes, where

SLALOM COURSE

the player who navigates the slalom course in the least number of strokes is the winner.

Both methods may be combined, so that if there is a tie for lowest number strokes, the player with the fastest time is the winner.

The player moves his ball in the direction of the arrows, around all aiming sticks and back to the start/finish line.

Starting / Finish line

SNEAK ATTACK

Overview: Sneak Attack is the opposite of "Catch Me (If You Can)," and helps develop distance control and feel for all types of shots, including putting, chipping, pitching, bunkers, and even full shots. The object is simple: hit each ball as close as possible to the prior ball without going past – in other words, "sneak up" on the prior ball..

Equipment Required:

✓ Supply of golf balls (either regular balls or range balls)
✓ 2 ball markers or tees

Setup: Please refer to the drawing on the facing page.

➢ Create a starting point by placing 2 ball markers or tees 6 feet apart either on the green (for putting) or in an area suitable for chipping, pitching, bunkers or full shots.

➢ Create an out-of-bounds limit or maximum distance that the first ball can travel. For putting, this could be the edge of the green, a string stretched across the green, or some other area. For chipping, pitching, and bunkers, this could be a line about 25 yards away from the starting point. For full shots it could be a yardage marker.

How To Play:

➢ The goal is to hit as many balls in a row as possible where no ball travels farther than the prior ball ("target ball"). Each ball must "sneak up" on the target ball.

➢ Begin by hitting the first ball as far as possible, without going over the out-of-bounds limit. That ball becomes the target ball for the next shot.

➢ Hit each subsequent ball, trying to come as close as possible to the prior ball. Each ball that stops short of the prior ball scores a point and that ball becomes the new target ball for the next shot.

➢ If a ball touches or goes farther than the target ball, the game ends.

SNEAK ATTACK

➤ Continue hitting until a ball either touches the target ball or goes farther than the target ball. Score a point each time the ball stops short of the target ball.

➤ If playing individually, keep a record of the number of points you score, and attempt to set a new record each time you play the game.

➤ If competing with multiple players, the winner is the player with the most points, once all players have had an equal number of turns.

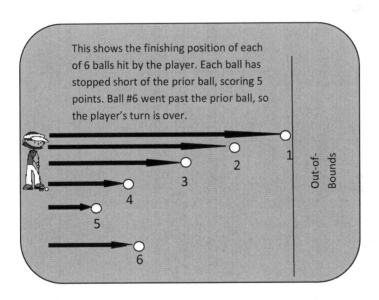

This shows the finishing position of each of 6 balls hit by the player. Each ball has stopped short of the prior ball, scoring 5 points. Ball #6 went past the prior ball, so the player's turn is over.

STRIPER

Overview: The direction your ball goes is determined by three simple factors that are true for all shots, from short putts to long drives. First and most important is the direction the face is looking as it contacts the ball. Always remember that the ball wants to go where the face is looking. We want the face to be square to your target, or looking directly where you want your ball to go as it leaves the face. And, remember that your target is not always the hole, to allow for break or other factors.

Second is the direction the face is traveling – is it moving straight toward the target at impact, or is it cutting across the target line either from inside to out or outside to in?

Third is the centeredness of contact, or hitting the ball on the "sweet spot." Your goal is to control all three of these factors when you hit a golf ball.

Striper is a great test of your ability to achieve this goal while putting. If you can do it, you will putt your ball with a true roll (no sidespin) right where you are aimed. Striper is a simple way to find out how successful you are at these three factors.

Equipment Required:

✓ One regular golf ball, specially prepared with a thick stripe around the entire ball (see drawing).

Setup: Please refer to the drawing on the facing page.

➢ Locate a flat surface of the putting green with no break. There does not need to be a hole; in fact, it is better to roll the ball about 10 feet in a flat open area on the green.

How To Play:

Place the striped ball on the green with the stripe aligned straight up and down. Aim the stripe in the direction you wish to roll the ball, where the green is flat. When you address the ball, line up your putter with the

STRIPER

stripe on the ball and putt the ball a short distance (for example 8-10 feet). There is no need to putt toward a hole; just aim for an open space in a flat area of the green. If you keep the putter face square, swing "down the line" and hit the putt on center, the ball will roll true and the stripe will remain straight up. If not, the ball will spin sideways and the stripe will wobble or spin.

Keep practicing Striper until you can roll ten perfect stripes in a row. If you can roll the stripe you will make those short putts.

THREES

Overview: Threes is a putting game that might require some athletic ability! Threes rewards 1-putts and penalizes 3-putts and will keep you and friends practicing your putting for hours.

Equipment Required:

✓ No special equipment is required

Setup: No special setup is required

How To Play:

Threes is played on the putting green with putts of any length. Players take turns choosing the starting point and the target hole. Each player uses three balls and putts each one from a starting point into a designated hole on the putting green.

If a ball is holed in one putt, it earns one credit that can be used to pay for a three-putt. If a ball is holed in two putts, no problem. If a ball is three-putted (or more), the player has two ways to pay for the error.

The player can use a one-putt credit as payment for the three- putt. If the player has no one-putt credits, he or she must do three push-ups. The payment has to be made immediately, and once a one-putt credit is used to pay for a three-putt, it is no longer usable for future three-putts.

THREES

THREE STRIKES

Overview: This game of elimination for 2-6 players helps develop:

- ✓ Direction and distance control
- ✓ Consistency

Equipment Required:

- ✓ Up to 6 ParKit Golf cones (1 per player)
- ✓ 1 ParKit Golf colored golf ball for each player
- ✓ 1 ParKit Golf 18-inch ring

Setup: Please refer to the drawing on the facing page.

- ➤ Place the ParZone ring around a hole on the putting or chipping green. The instructor may use judgment and use a larger ring based on the skill level of the players.

- ➤ Create a chipping station for each player by placing 1 ParKit cone in a flat area appropriate for chipping up to 30 yards. Each player should have a similar lie and angle to the ring.

- ➤ Each player will use their own white ball, plus a different colored ParKit ball.

How To Play:

- ➤ Players go to their chipping stations and prepare to chip their own white ball (ensure balls are marked for identification).

- ➤ The instructor will announce "1-2-3... CHIP", and all players will chip at the same time.

- ➤ The player whose ball is the farthest white ball from the hole gets a strike (ParKit colored balls do not count for strikes). Any player who chips into the ring or hole subtracts 1 strike from his total (the minimum strike count is zero).

- ➤ When a player gets 3 strikes, he is "out" and must change to his ParKit colored ball for subsequent chipping rounds. The player

THREE STRIKES

then continues chipping in subsequent rounds, but his colored ball does not count in the measuring for strikes.

➤ If a player who is "out" chips into the ring or hole with a colored ball, he changes back to a white ball with 2 strikes and continues competing in subsequent rounds.

➤ The game is over when there is only one player using a white ball for the start of the next round; that player is the winner.

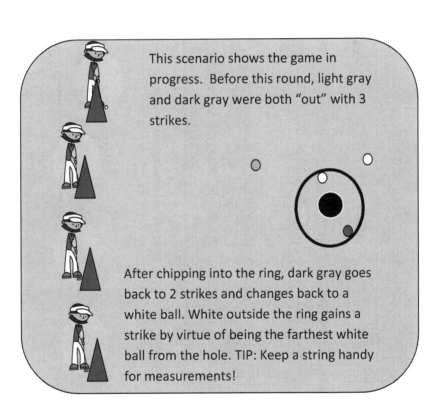

This scenario shows the game in progress. Before this round, light gray and dark gray were both "out" with 3 strikes.

After chipping into the ring, dark gray goes back to 2 strikes and changes back to a white ball. White outside the ring gains a strike by virtue of being the farthest white ball from the hole. TIP: Keep a string handy for measurements!

TIC TAC GOLF

Overview: This version of classic tic-tac-toe is great for putting or other short game situations and may be played individually or in teams (teams need not be of equal size). Tic Tac Golf helps to develop:

- ✓ Accuracy and distance control
- ✓ Strategy

Equipment Required:

- ✓ 4 ParKit Golf cones
- ✓ 15 ParKit Golf colored golf balls
- ✓ ParKit Golf colored string OR 9 3' ParZone rings

Setup: Please refer to the drawing on the facing page.

➢ Create a starting point by placing 2 ParKit cones 6 feet apart in a flat area appropriate for pitching up to 20 yards.

➢ Place the other ParKit cones where players will await their turn.

➢ Create a tic-tac-toe grid by marking 3' X 3' squares with string, turf paint, or chalk. Or, use 9 3' ParZone rings arranged as shown to make the grid.

How To Play:

➢ Choose sides and play individually with two players, or create two teams (need not be equal sized). Give one side 15 ParKit colored golf balls. The other side will use either white balls or range balls. Determine which side is to play first.

➢ The game is played like the classic tic-tac-toe. Taking turns, each side attempts to hit a ball into a square on the Tic Tac Golf grid. The first side to pitch into a square claims that square for the side. Claim the square for the side by leaving the player's ball in the square.

TIC TAC GOLF

➤ Retrieve and re-use balls as needed to maintain a supply of balls for each team.

➤ The winner is the first side to make 3 in a row, column, or diagonal (as with tic-tac-toe).

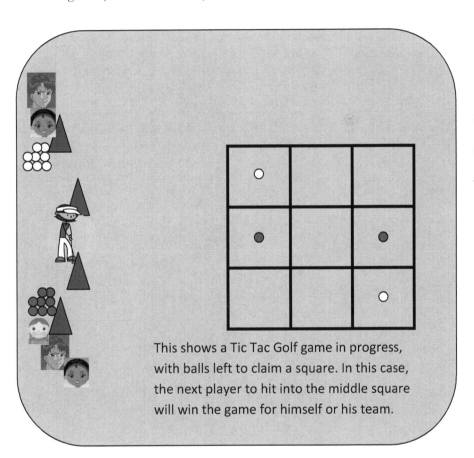

This shows a Tic Tac Golf game in progress, with balls left to claim a square. In this case, the next player to hit into the middle square will win the game for himself or his team.

TIC TAC GOLF

Setup Variation: An easier way to set up Tic Tac Golf is to use 9 3' ParZone rings instead of making the grid with string. Simply place the rings on the putting green as shown on the facing page. Balls coming to rest within a ring claim that "square" for Tic Tac Golf.

How to Play Variation: A fun and exciting variation on the rules is to allow "knock-outs." With this format, if a player's ball comes to rest within a square that has been claimed by another side, the player's ball replaces the existing ball, claiming the square for the player's side and knocking the other side out of that square. This forces the teams to strategize on where to put their ball and makes for a fun "give and take" nature to the game.

If a ball strikes a ball that is in a square, the ball that was struck is replaced in the square unless the striking ball also comes to rest in that square. If the striking ball comes to rest in another square, it claims that square.

This variation works well with up to six teams of any number of players. Players must alternate taking turns for their team, and only four colored balls are needed for each team (just make sure that each team has a different color). Establish tee markers using ParKit cones for each side. Place the tee markers close to the grid for beginners and farther away for more skilled players.

TIC TAC GOLF

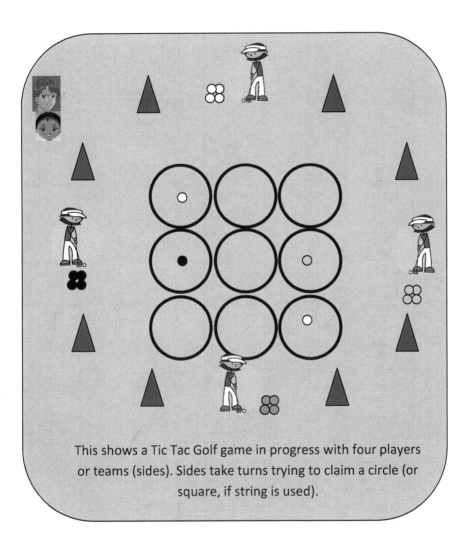

This shows a Tic Tac Golf game in progress with four players or teams (sides). Sides take turns trying to claim a circle (or square, if string is used).

TOWER OF POWER

<u>Overview</u>: This game for 2 or more players helps develop:

- ✓ Full swing aim
- ✓ Ball trajectory control
- ✓ Instinctive shotmaking, without becoming preoccupied with technique

Equipment Required:

- ✓ 5 ParKit Golf cones
- ✓ ParKit Golf scoring pad
- ✓ 6 or more plastic range ball baskets (not in ParKit kit)

Setup: Please refer to the drawing on the facing page.

- ➢ Make two full swing stations by placing three ParKit cones in line about 6 feet apart on the practice tee suitable for full driver shots. Place a supply of golf balls in each station.

- ➢ Place one ParKit cone for each team, where players will await their turn.

- ➢ Construct the "tower of power" by stacking the plastic range ball baskets on top of one another in a pyramid as shown. WARNING: DO NOT USE METAL RANGE BASKETS FOR THIS GAME!

How To Play:

- Create two teams (need not be equal sized). Each team will determine its order of play. Players wait behind their "on-deck" cone until it is their turn.

- One student from each team will enter their hitting station. When the instructor says "GO", both players will hit 5 balls at the "tower of power". The goal is to knock the tower down. The first player to knock down part or all of the tower earns a point for their team.

TOWER OF POWER

- After the first round of players have hit 5 balls, they return to the "on deck" area and the next player from each team takes a turn.

- If a player hits more than one ball at a time, he loses the round and the other team gets one point.

- The winner is the team with the most points after all players have had a turn.

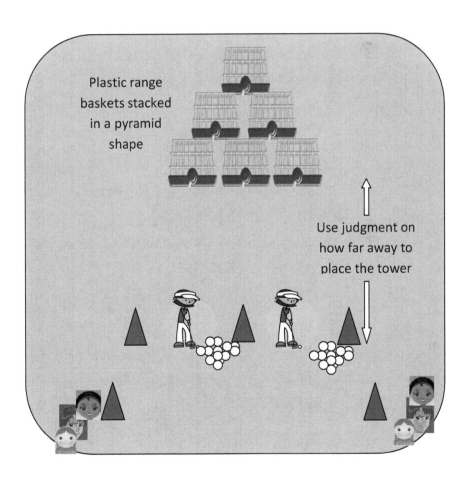

Plastic range baskets stacked in a pyramid shape

Use judgment on how far away to place the tower

VIRTUAL GOLF

Overview: This game for two or more players helps develop:

- ✓ Full swing shotmaking technique
- ✓ Club selection and shot strategy
- ✓ Etiquette in order of play
- ✓ Rules in dealing with hazards, out-of-bounds, etc.

Equipment Required:

- ✓ 1-2 ParKit Golf cones
- ✓ 2 ParKit Golf aiming sticks
- ✓ ParKit Golf scoring pad

Setup: Please refer to the drawing on the facing page.

- ➢ Make a full swing station by aligning two ParKit aiming sticks about 6 feet apart on the practice tee suitable for full shots. Place a supply of golf balls in the station.

- ➢ Place one ParKit cone where players will await their turn.

- ➢ Use your imagination to describe a golf hole as viewed from the full swing station. Describe the fairway, any imaginary bunkers, trees, dogleg shape, hazards, and green location. Players will "play" this "hole", so ensure each player understands your vision of the hole.

How To Play:

- Determine the order of play. Players wait behind the "on-deck" cone until it is their turn.

- Following the order of play, each player will select a club and "tee off" on the imaginary hole, remembering where their ball comes to rest.

- After each player has teed off, players will prepare to hit their second shot. Based on the location of their tee shot and following the rules of golf, each player will select a new club appropriate for

VIRTUAL GOLF

their next shot and play the "hole" as described by the instructor, always hitting from the full swing station. Play continues until all players are "on the green".

- The winner is the player to reach the imaginary "green" in the least number of shots.

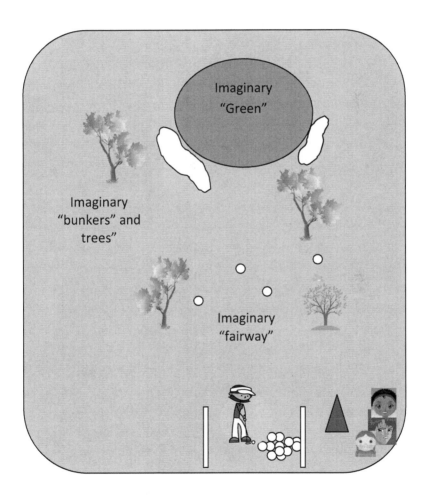

WHAM BOX

Overview: Wham Box provides great motivation to hit shot after shot with controlled trajectory, laser accuracy, and excellent ball contact. Everyone loves destroying things, and Wham Box caters to that innate desire.

Equipment Required:

- ✓ 1 empty golf club set box, or other tall, wide cardboard box
- ✓ Large supply of range balls

Setup: Please refer to the drawing on the facing page.

➢ Find an isolated spot on the driving range suitable for full shots of up to 150 yards.

➢ Create a hitting station with a large supply of range balls.

➢ Place an empty golf club set box or other large, tall or wide cardboard box on the range approximately 20 yards in front of the starting staion.

➢ For extra fun, allow the students to get creative and draw faces, targets, or other fun things on the box.

➢ Pour 20-30 range balls into the box to help hold it upright and keep it from being knocked down by wind, then close the top.

➢ Create teams of any size, or play individually.

How To Play:

The object of the game is to destroy the box by hitting it with golf balls. Players take turns hitting a ball at the box. Use fun and judgment in allowing players to win "points" for hitting the box, hitting a target on the box, or other achievement. Players should experiment with different clubs and shot techniques to find the best combination for hitting powerful, low trajectory, accurate shots.

WHAM BOX

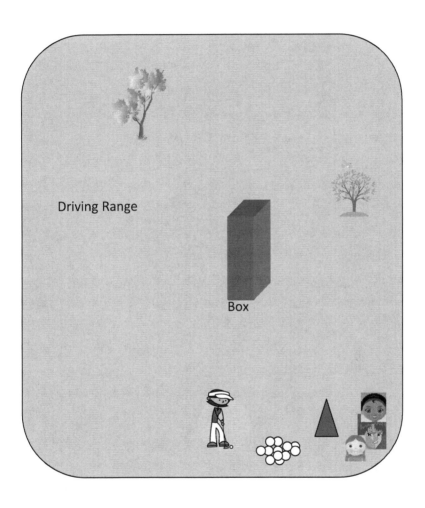

WICKET TRAIL

Overview: Wicket Trail helps visualize breaks, or slopes, on the green and helps understand how putts break. The object is to arrange wickets on the green so that you can putt through them to the hole.

Equipment Required:

    ✓ 5 ParKit Golf Wickets (large 1 point wickets)
    ✓ 2 ball markers

Setup: Please refer to the drawing on the facing page.

➤ Choose a spot on the practice putting green with some slope that will produce a breaking putt.

➤ Place the two ball markers about 6" apart on the green, about 10 feet away from the hole. Place your ball between the markers.

➤ Survey the putt and estimate the curvature of the putt. Mark your expected putting line by inserting each wicket into the putting green. Arrange the wickets in a curved line representing the line you think your ball must follow to reach the hole.

How To Play:

➤ The object of the game is to putt your ball through all five wickets and into the hole in the least number of tries.

➤ Begin by putting from between the ball markers toward the first wicket with enough speed to reach the hole.

➤ If your ball goes through each wicket and into the hole, the game is over. If the ball does not go through each wicket, try the putt again, and reset the wickets as needed. Use your best judgment of the line of the putt to reset only those wickets that need to be moved in order to mark the line of the putt to the hole.

➤ If the game seems too easy, start farther from the hole or select a putt across a more severe slope.

WICKET TRAIL

➢ Keep a record of the number of tries you require to make the putt while passing through each wicket, and attempt to set a new record each time you play the game.

➢ If competing with multiple players, the winner is the first player to hole the putt while passing through each wicket.

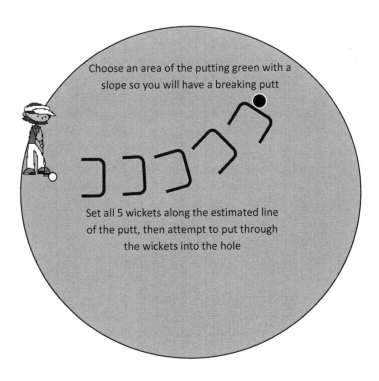

Choose an area of the putting green with a slope so you will have a breaking putt

Set all 5 wickets along the estimated line of the putt, then attempt to put through the wickets into the hole

NOTES

NOTES

NOTES

ABOUT THE AUTHORS

The ParKit Golf Team is Diana Law and PGA members Don Law, Rick Heard, and Bill Scott. Our team members have won many PGA awards and professional designations. ParKit's products and games are the centerpiece of many golf instruction programs, including the U.S. Kids Golf Instructor Certification Program.

Rick Heard is a PGA teaching professional and co-owner of the Don Law Golf Academy in Boca Raton, Florida. A PGA member since 2002, Rick was president of the Southeast Chapter of the South Florida Section PGA for six years ending in 2012, and was awarded the chapter's Golf Professional of the Year award for 2010. Rick also received the 2002 chapter Junior Golf Leader award and the Southeast Chapter PGA Horton Smith education award for both 2007 and 2008. Rick is a U.S. Kids Certified Kids Instructor and a U.S. Kids Top 50 Kids Teacher. Rick is also the author of **Daddy Caddy on the Bag**, a coaching guide for parents, and **Daddy Caddy Off the Bag**, a self-improvement guide for kids.

Don Law has been a PGA member since 1993 and a teaching professional and director of instruction since 1995. A highly decorated professional, Don was awarded the 2012 National Junior Golf Leader of the Year award by the PGA of America, and was recently inducted into the South Florida PGA Hall of Fame. Don has received 14 PGA chapter and section awards, including the 2011 Golf Professional of the Year in the South Florida PGA Section. He is also a US Kids Master Instructor.

Bill Scott has been a PGA member since 1997 and has been a teaching professional at the Don Law Golf Academy since 2004. Bill is a U.S. Kids Golf Certified Instructor, a U.S. Kids Golf Top 50 Kids

Teacher and a U.S. Kids Golf Master Instructor. Bill won the 2006, 2007, and 2010 Southeast Chapter PGA Junior Golf Leader and the 2011 and 2013 South Florida Section PGA Junior Golf Leader Awards. He was also the 2012 Southeast Chapter PGA Teacher of the Year.

Diana Law is the inspiration and energy behind just about everything any of us have accomplished, and she is the prime motivator for ParKit Golf, Inc.

The Don Law Golf Academy specializes in teaching juniors, and has hundreds of young golfers in its classes and camps in four South Florida locations. The DLGA also has a full suite of expert instructional programs for adults of all abilities.

Made in the USA
Middletown, DE
10 June 2015